100

Science Words
Every College
Graduate
Should Know

100
Science Words
Every College
Graduate
Should Know

THE 100 WORDS™ *From the Editors of the*
AMERICAN HERITAGE®
DICTIONARIES

HOUGHTON MIFFLIN
Boston   New York

No part of this work may be reproduced or transmitted in any form or by any means, electronic or mechanical, including photocopying and recording, or by any information storage or retrieval system without the prior written permission of Houghton Mifflin Company unless such copying is expressly permitted by federal copyright law. Address inquiries to Reference Permissions, Houghton Mifflin Company, 222 Berkeley Street, Boston, MA 02116.

Visit our websites: www.ahdictionary.com *or*
www.houghtonmifflinbooks.com

LIBRARY OF CONGRESS CATALOGING-IN-PUBLICATION DATA
100 science words every college graduate should know : the 100 words / from the editors of the American heritage dictionaries.
    p. cm.
 ISBN-13: 978-0-618-70174-2
 ISBN-10: 0-618-70174-5
 1. Science--Dictionaries. I. Title: One hundred science words every college graduate should know. II. Houghton Mifflin Company.
 Q123.A15 2006
 503--dc22

                                                                    2005033569

Text design by Anne Chalmers

MANUFACTURED IN THE UNITED STATES OF AMERICA

QUM 10 9 8 7 6 5 4 3 2 1

Notes illustration: **feather and flask design** Martha Kennedy
A-Z entry illustrations: **capacitor** UG/GGS Information Services, **centripetal force** Precision Graphics, **Fibonacci sequence** Elizabeth Morales, **fission** Precision Graphics, **imaginary number** and **mitochondrion** Elizabeth Morales, **monotreme** Cecile Duray-Bito, **orbital** Elizabeth Morales, **refraction** Jerry Malone, and **xerophyte** Chris Costello

Preface

This book takes its place in the series of "100 Words" books assembled by the editors of the American Heritage Dictionaries. The books share a common purpose: to challenge readers to develop a more sophisticated vocabulary. Thus *100 Words Every High School Graduate Should Know* presents vocabulary that a well-rounded student should have encountered and presumably mastered by the time of graduation. The next book in the series, *100 Words Every High School Freshman Should Know,* does the same thing for students finishing middle school. Other books in the series highlight 100 of the most commonly confused and misused words and 100 words that lovers of words will find irresistibly dear to their hearts.

This book presents 100 words in science that every college graduate, regardless of major or specialization, ought to know. The words were selected because they represent the kind of vocabulary that a person who is literate in science should understand. The words are not the most fundamental scientific terms that are the substance of textbooks. Rather, the editors have sought out words that are both essential to understanding science's powerful explanations and interesting in their own right.

These words come from a wide variety of fields — from subatomic physics to genetics to botany and medicine — and they are all words that a scientifically aware layperson will encounter in reading. For this reason, the editors have done much more than compile a list of dictionary definitions. Instead, we have written expansive explanations of each word's meaning and importance, and in some cases, its history. A series of feature paragraphs includes fascinating additional information that will spur inquisitive minds to learn more.

For most people, science is largely an assembly of words, words that organize the continuum of experience and the behavior of the universe into discrete and identifiable parts, processes, and relationships. Understanding some of these words necessarily entails understanding others. For those interested in the vocabulary of science, the universe is always expanding. This little book offers a point in space from which to continue making observations.

— Joseph P. Pickett,
Executive Editor

Note on Etymologies

Etymologies appear in square brackets following the last definition. A language name, linguistic form (in italics), and brief definition of the form are given for each stage of the derivation presented. For reasons of space, the etymologies sometimes omit certain stages in the derivation of words with long and complex histories whenever this omission does not significantly detract from a broad understanding of the word's history. To avoid redundancy, a language, form, or definition is not repeated if it is identical to the corresponding item in the immediately preceding stage. The word *from* is used to indicate origin of any kind: by inheritance, borrowing, abbreviation, the addition of affixes, or any other linguistic process. When an etymology shows the parts of a compound word, a colon introduces this section of the etymology, and a plus sign (+) separates each word part from the next. Occasionally, a form is given that is not actually preserved in written documents, but that scholars are confident did exist — such a form is marked by an asterisk (*). Many of the etymologies in this book use the term *New Latin*, which refers to the variety of Latin used as an international medium of communication among scientists, physicians, and other scholars since around AD 1500. The term *Latin* itself, when not further modified, is reserved for the form of Latin used in classical antiquity, until about AD 200.

Pronunciation Guide

Pronunciations appear in parentheses after some bold-face entry words. If a word has more than one pronunciation, the first pronunciation is usually more common than the other, but often they are equally common. Pronunciations are shown after inflections and related words where necessary.

Stress is the relative degree of emphasis that a word's syllables are spoken with. An unmarked syllable has the weakest stress in the word. The strongest, or primary, stress is indicated with a bold mark ($'$). A lighter mark ($'$) indicates a secondary level of stress. The stress mark follows the syllable it applies to. Words of one syllable have no stress mark because there is no other stress level that the syllable is compared to.

The key on page xi shows the pronunciation symbols used in this book. To the right of the symbols are words that show how the symbols are pronounced. The letters whose sound corresponds to the symbols are shown in boldface.

The symbol (ə) is called *schwa*. It represents a vowel with the weakest level of stress in a word. The schwa sound varies slightly according to the vowel it represents or the sounds around it:

abundant (ə-bŭn′dənt)   **moment** (mō′mənt)

civil (sĭv′əl)   **grateful** (grāt′fəl)

PRONUNCIATION KEY

Symbol	Examples	Symbol	Examples
ă	pat	oi	noise
ā	pay	ŏŏ	took
âr	care	ŏŏr	lure
ä	father	ōō	boot
b	bib	ou	out
ch	church	p	pop
d	deed, milled	r	roar
ĕ	pet	s	sauce
ē	bee	sh	ship, dish
f	fife, phase, rough	t	tight, stopped
		th	thin
g	gag	*th*	this
h	hat	ŭ	cut
hw	which	ûr	urge, term, firm, word, heard
ĭ	pit		
ī	pie, by		
îr	deer, pier	v	valve
j	judge	w	with
k	kick, cat, pique	y	yes
l	lid, needle	z	zebra, xylem
m	mum	zh	vision, pleasure, garage
n	no, sudden		
ng	thing		
ŏ	pot	ə	about, item, edible, gallop, circus
ō	toe		
ô	caught, paw		
ôr	core	ər	butter

THE MOTION OF STILLNESS

The temperature of a substance is related to the motion of its molecules. The more they move, the warmer the substance. The motion of molecules, furthermore, gives them kinetic energy. At **absolute zero,** molecules have what is called zero-point energy: minimal kinetic energy. No heat energy can be extracted from them, but the molecules are not, strictly speaking, motionless. The uncertainty principle of quantum mechanics entails that the atoms cannot have both a definite position and zero momentum at the same time, so the molecules of a substance, even at absolute zero, are always, in a sense, "wiggling."

absolute zero

The lowest possible temperature, at which all molecules have the least possible amount of kinetic energy. Absolute zero is equal to 0 K, –459.67°F, or –273.15°C.

At temperatures approaching absolute zero, the physical characteristics of some substances change significantly. For example, some substances change from electrical insulators to conductors, while others change from conductors to insulators. Absolute zero has never been reached in laboratory experiments, but using laser traps and other techniques, scientists at the Massachusetts Institute of Technology have been able to cool rubidium atoms to 2×10^{-9} kelvins.

[**ABSOLUTE:** From Latin *absolūtus,* unrestricted, past participle of *absolvere,* to absolve : *ab-,* away + *solvere,* to loosen (ultimately from Proto-Indo-European **swe-,* self, and **leu-,* loosen, also the source of English *loose* and *lose*). **ZERO:** From Italian *zero,* alteration of Medieval Latin *zephirum,* from Arabic *ṣifr,* nothing (translation of Sanskrit *śūnyam*, void, zero), from *ṣafira,* to be empty, from the Proto-Semitic root **ṣpr.*]

agoraphobia (ăg′ər-ə-fō′bē-ə *or* ə-gôr′ə-fō′bē-ə)

An abnormal fear of open or public places.

Most people don't give a second thought to attending a concert, standing in line at an amusement park, or reading in a crowded waiting room. For people with agoraphobia, however, these situations can trigger intense symptoms of anxiety, including dizziness, chest pain, and trembling. Agoraphobia is a *phobic disorder,* that is, a disorder in which individuals experience persistent and irrational fears that are not caused by physical disease or drugs. People with agoraphobia have attacks of anxiety or panic in public situations, which they consequently try to avoid. In severe cases, some people cannot leave their homes. It is the anticipatory fear of having an anxiety attack in situations that are unfamiliar, unpredictable, or not easily escaped that incapacitates people with agoraphobia. One could say they are anxious about becoming anxious.

Agoraphobia is surprisingly common, affecting almost 4 percent of women and almost 2 percent of men. The usual treatment is with *desensitization* or *exposure therapy,* in which the person is introduced to and then gradually exposed to a feared situation with professional support.

[From Greek *agorā,* marketplace + Late Latin *-phobia,* fear (from Greek *-phobiā,* from *phobos,* fear).]

alga (ăl′gə)
Plural: algae (ăl′jē)

Any of various photosynthetic organisms that often live in water, ranging in size from single cells to large spreading seaweeds.

The word *alga* serves as a convenient catch-all term for a variety of organisms, including cyanobacteria, green algae, brown algae, and red algae, that sometimes have a plantlike appearance and that in aquatic environments are often the primary source of food for organisms that cannot perform photosynthesis. However, the various groups of organisms called *algae* in fact differ markedly in their genetic makeup, in the chemical composition of their bodies, and in their reproductive life cycles. These differences indicate that the groups are quite distinct from each other when viewed from an evolutionary perspective.

The photosynthetic organisms formerly called *blue-green algae* are now classified as bacteria and usually called *cyanobacteria.* The group called *green algae* is familiar from such organisms as *Spirogyra,* often seen as filamentous pond scum, and *Ulva,* or sea lettuce, often washed up on beaches. *Brown algae* such as kelp are mostly found in marine waters, and the Sargasso Sea is known for its floating masses of the brown alga *Sargassum.* The red pigments of the group called *red algae* absorb the blue-green wavelengths of light that reach the deeper coastal waters where they live. However, the phenomena called *red tides* (blooms of toxic algae that kill fish and contaminate beds of shellfish) are not caused by red algae. Instead, they are usually caused by an unrelated group of mostly unicellular organisms called *dinoflagellates.*

[From Latin *alga,* seaweed.]

ALGORITHMS AT WORK

Computers are constantly executing **algorithms**. The creation of efficient algorithms is vital to applications in which difficult computational tasks must be performed quickly, as for example in the cryptography used to conceal private information such as credit card numbers during Internet transactions. Credit card companies encrypt and decrypt thousands of numbers every second, and for this, specialized algorithms have been developed. In fact, in many countries, newly devised algorithms can be patented.

4

algorithm (ăl′gə-rĭth′əm)

*A finite set of unambiguous instructions that, given some set of
initial conditions, can be performed in a prescribed sequence to
achieve a certain goal and that has a recognizable set of end
conditions.*

An example of an algorithm is the procedure we learn in
school for adding numbers on paper. The *initial conditions*
consist in having the numbers written one above the other,
decimal places in line. The *instructions* to be followed in sequence involve adding numbers in a column, starting at the
right, writing the sum underneath in the same column, carrying digits if necessary. The *goal* is to have the sum written
below the numbers, and the *end condition* is to have added or
carried all of the digits. Similarly, to follow a recipe or the instructions for building a model plane is to follow an algorithm.

[Variant (influenced by *arithmetic*) of *algorism*, the decimal system,
from Medieval Latin *algorismus*, after Muhammad ibn-Musa *al-
Khwārizmi*, "The Khwarcsmian," Persian mathematician and astronomer whose works introduced Arabic numerals to Western
mathematics, from Persian *Khwārazm*, area near the Aral Sea.]

5 allele (ə-lēl′)

Any of the possible forms in which a gene for a specific trait can occur.

A *gene* is a hereditary unit that determines a specific trait (called a *character*) of an organism. In almost all animal cells, an allele, or type of a given gene, is inherited from each parent. Each allele resides on one of two paired chromosomes. Paired alleles that are the same are called *homozygous* and those that are different are called *heterozygous.*

In heterozygous pairings, one allele is usually *dominant,* and the other is *recessive.* A dominant allele will express its trait when paired with a recessive allele or another dominant allele. A recessive allele must be paired with another recessive allele for its trait to be manifest. Complex traits such as height and longevity are usually produced by the interactions of numerous pairs of alleles.

[From German *Allel,* short for *Allelomorph,* allele, from English *allelomorph,* ultimately from Greek *allēlōn,* mutually (from *allos,* other) + Greek *morphē,* shape.]

6 alternating current

An electric current that repeatedly changes its direction or strength, usually at a certain frequency or range of frequencies.

Power stations generate alternating current because it is easy to raise and lower the voltage of such current using *transformers.* Transformers use the magnetic field generated by the current in one coil of wire to induce a voltage in another coil. However, a static magnetic field can't induce a voltage—the field must be *changing* in order for a voltage to arise. Alternating current in one coil, since it is always changing back and forth, makes the magnetic field change too, so voltage arises in the other coil. This makes alternating current vital to the efficient transmission of electrical power: the voltage can be raised very high for transmission, since high voltages lose less power as heat than low voltages do, and then lowered to levels safer for domestic and industrial use. In North America, the frequency of alternation is 60 hertz, or 60 cycles per second. In most other parts of the world, it is 50 hertz.

The term *alternating current* is also used to describe alternating voltages or power, especially when used with the abbreviation AC. It stands in contrast with *direct current,* or DC (also used of voltages and power), which does not significantly change in direction or strength.

amygdala (ə-mĭg′də-lə)
Plural: **amygdalae** (ə-mĭg′də-lē)

A small almond-shaped mass of gray matter found in the brain and essential to the expression of anger, pleasure, and other emotions.

The amygdala is found in the front part of each *temporal lobe,* a portion of the brain that controls hearing and aspects of language perception, emotion, and memory. The amygdala is a part of the *limbic system,* a group of structures with connections to the nervous and endocrine systems involved in sleep, sexual arousal, emotion, and the processing of memory. The amygdala's role lies in the expression of and nonverbal response to emotion. Feelings and displays of aggression, rage, defensiveness, anxiety, and some pleasurable emotions result from neurological and hormonal activation by the amygdala. These include characteristic facial expressions and physiological changes such as sweaty palms. The amygdala is also part of the *olfactory system,* which regulates the sense of smell. Thus, odors can elicit powerful memories and emotions.

[From Latin *amygdala,* almond, from Greek *amugdalē.*]

anaphylaxis (ăn′ə-fə-lăk′sĭs)

A sudden, life-threatening allergic reaction, characterized by dilation of blood vessels and contraction of smooth muscle tissue.

Anaphylaxis is caused by a secondary exposure to a foreign substance. The substance acts as an *antigen,* provoking a preliminary immune response with the first exposure and causing an immediate and full-blown response (known as an *immediate hypersensitivity reaction*) with the second. Blood products, drugs, and insect stings are among the antigens that can result in anaphylactic reactions. Susceptibility to anaphylaxis and other allergic disorders is typically inherited.

In milder cases, blood-vessel dilation causes a drop in blood pressure, along with hives or skin swelling. Contraction of involuntary muscle causes bronchial spasms with shortness of breath and gastrointestinal symptoms such as nausea and diarrhea. Untreated symptoms can lead to *anaphylactic shock,* causing failure of the circulatory system that can be fatal. Emergency treatment with injection of the drug *epinephrine* is given to prevent anaphylactic shock.

[Ultimately from Greek *ana,* up + *phulaxis,* guarding (from *phulassein,* to guard, from *phulax,* guard).]

9

angiogenesis (ăn′jē-ō-jĕn′ĭ-sĭs)
Plural: **angiogeneses** (ăn′jē-ō-jĕn′ĭ-sēz′)

The formation of new blood vessels, especially those that supply cancerous tissues.

The process of angiogenesis occurs naturally in the body as a way of healing wounds and replenishing the blood flow to injured tissues. The growth of blood vessels is regulated by natural substances in the body that either stimulate or inhibit angiogenesis. In a healthy person, these substances are maintained in a balance that meets the body's needs.

In 1971, Dr. Judah Folkman published a theory that the growth of malignant tumors is dependent upon cancer cells secreting angiogenic substances. He postulated that the new blood vessels supply oxygen and nutrients and remove wastes, allowing the cancerous tissue to survive and facilitating the entrance of tumor cells into the bloodstream. Interestingly, he noted that the presence of tumor cells in other organs, or *metastases,* sometimes becomes apparent only after the removal of a large primary tumor. This phenomenon provided evidence that tumors also secrete angiogenesis inhibitors that keep metastases from getting larger once they have entered the bloodstream.

These novel ideas led to the development of numerous synthetic *angiogenesis inhibitors* that are currently being tested in clinical trials. The first drug in this class was approved by the FDA for use in patients with colorectal cancer in 2004. Different drugs that stimulate angiogenesis have also been tested in patients who need blood restored to organs that have been damaged by coronary artery disease, stroke, and other vascular diseases.

[From New Latin *angiogenesis* : Greek *angeio-*, vessel, blood vessel (from *angeion*, diminutive of *angos*, vessel) + *genesis*, production, generation (from Proto-Indo-European **genə-*, to beget, give birth, also the source of English *kin* and *kind*).]

apoptosis (ăp′əp-tō′sĭs *or* ăp′ə-tō′sĭs)

A natural process of self-destruction in certain cells that are damaged or genetically programmed to have a limited life span.

Apoptosis, also called *programmed cell death,* is an orderly series of events by which organisms get rid of injured or unnecessary cells. These cells essentially commit suicide to ensure the survival and normal function of the organism. Certain drugs, radiation, misfolded proteins, and other harmful influences can cause cells to become cancerous or otherwise toxic, and such cells can harm the organism if they are not destroyed. In addition, some cells, such as red blood cells or certain skin cells, have naturally short life spans that are terminated by apoptosis. Cells that exist temporarily in the development of an organism, such as the tail of a tadpole when it becomes a frog or the tissue between fetal fingers that disappears before birth, are also eliminated by apoptosis. Here, improper apoptosis can cause birth defects and disease.

During apoptosis, the cell shrinks, and enzymes destroy mitochondria and the contents of the nucleus. The cell then disintegrates into small membrane-bound particles that are engulfed by *phagocytes,* white blood cells that digest waste products. Three mechanisms are thought to trigger cell death: internal damage that signals the release of the degradative enzymes, the binding of chemical "death activators" to receptors on the surface of the cell, and the release of *apoptosis-inducing factor,* a protein normally contained in mitochondria, that moves into the nucleus and binds to and destroys the cell's DNA.

[From New Latin *apoptōsis*, from Greek, a falling away : *apo*, away from (from Proto-Indo-European **apo-*, also the source of English *of* and *off*) + *ptōsis*, a fall (from *piptein*, *ptō-*, to fall, from Proto-Indo-European **pteə-*, to fly, also the source of English *feather*).]

archaeon (är′kē-ŏn′)
Plural: archaea (är′kē-ə)

Any of a group of unicellular microorganisms that resemble bacteria but are fundamentally different from bacteria in their genetic makeup as well as in the chemical structure of their cell walls and other characteristics.

Many archaea are *extremophiles,* inhabiting environments that are very hot, salty, or otherwise hostile to other forms of life, as for example hot mineral springs or deep-sea hydrothermal vents. Other archaea are found in less extreme environments such as animal digestive systems.

Until recently, scientists classified life into two large groups: the bacteria with their DNA free in the cell and the eukaryotes (such as plants, fungi, and animals) with their DNA contained in a nucleus. The organisms now classified as archaea had been classified among the bacteria, because their DNA is not gathered into a nucleus. In the 1970s, however, scientists took a closer look at some archaeal species and discovered that the genes of these organisms were quite different from those found in other bacteria. Archaeal DNA is also copied and "read" in ways that resemble those found in eukaryotes rather than those found in bacteria. In addition, archaeal cell walls are composed of substances different from those in bacterial cell walls.

These discoveries challenged earlier theories about the ultimate relationships between organisms in the family tree of life, and now many scientists have accepted a new classification of all life into three large groups or domains: the bacteria, the archaea, and the eukaryotes.

[From New Latin, from Greek *arkhaion,* neuter nominative-accusative singular of *arkhaios,* ancient (since many archaea thrive in environments without oxygen that resemble those believed to have existed on the early Earth).]

artesian well

A well drilled through impermeable rock or sediment into an underground layer that contains water under pressure.

Wells produce water because they are drilled into regions underground that contain porous material, such as sandstone or gravel, and are filled with water. Sometimes these regions, known as *aquifers,* contain water under pressure. If so, the aquifer is known as an *artesian aquifer,* and a well drilled into it is called an *artesian well.* Many artesian wells contain water under so much pressure that the water flows without the need for a pump, sometimes shooting high into the air.

Artesian aquifers are pressurized because the water in them is trapped between layers of impermeable rock or sediment. Since the layers of the Earth are usually tilted to some degree, one part of the aquifer is higher than the others and closer to the surface. Water can flow down into this area, known as the *recharge area.* Since the recharge area is higher than the confined area, the force of gravity causes pressure to build up in the aquifer. If a well is drilled in an area of the aquifer that is below the recharge area, the pressure will force the water to rise into the well.

[From French *artésien,* from Old French *artesien,* of Artois, from *Arteis,* Artois, France, where such a well was drilled in 1126 by Carthusian monks using new drilling technology.]

ATP

Short for adenosine triphosphate. *An organic compound,*
$C_{10}H_{16}N_5O_{13}P_3$, *that serves as a source of energy for many
metabolic processes in cells.*

Many nutrients, especially sugars and carbohydrates, are
used by our bodies as a kind of fuel. All living things burn
such fuels in chemical reactions that cells use to maintain
themselves, build proteins and other compounds, reproduce,
change shape or position, or move around. But these chemical reactions provide energy in the form of heat, which is
difficult to store for future use, especially within cells. Heat
has a further drawback for biological use in that most cellular processes require a fairly even temperature distribution
across the cell, so the generation of hot spots where reactions
produce sudden bursts of heat might hinder rather than abet
cellular activity.

Thus, for the cells of an organism to function in a manner
efficient enough to sustain life, the energy released by the
processing of nutrients must be stored in a form other than
heat. Biology has provided its own answer to this problem —
the chemical ATP. Energy produced by burning nutrients is
stored in a chemical bond of ATP, which acts as a chemical
energy battery.

Inside cells, ATP is built in the structures known as *mitochondria.* Here, nutrients such as sugars are used as raw material to add a third phosphate group to the chemical called
ADP (adenosine diphosphate). The ATP can be distributed
around the cell without disrupting other cell processes. The
energy of ATP is made available when it breaks back down
into ADP in a process called *hydrolysis,* which involves the
combination of a molecule of ATP with a water molecule.

TUNING IN,
THANKS TO BANDWIDTH

The more stations a radio can tune in, the wider its overall **bandwidth**. Similarly, the bandwidth of a wire that carries high frequency signals (as in a computer modem that transmits signals along telephone lines) ultimately determines how much information can be transmitted through that wire. The notion of bandwidth has therefore become very important in computer science and telecommunications, and the word has even acquired a second meaning as a result, referring to the amount of digital information transmitted per unit time.

14 bandwidth

1. *The numerical difference between a maximum and a minimum frequency, as of electromagnetic radiation or an electrical signal. It is measured in hertz (cycles per second), or in a multiple of hertz such as kilohertz or megahertz.*

The term *bandwidth* is often used in descriptions of media or devices that carry radiation or signals. The range of frequencies that can be tuned in by a radio receiver can be thought of as the bandwidth of the receiver. Electromagnetic radiation given off by natural phenomena may also be measured in terms of bandwidth; astronomers, for example, are interested in the bandwidth of x-ray radiation emitted by a supernova.

2. *The amount of digital information that can be passed along a communications channel in a given period of time, measured in bits per second (or more commonly a multiple thereof, as in kilobits or megabits per second).*

A *bit* is a single piece of information that has one of two possible values—one or zero. It is the smallest discrete unit of information, and from combinations of bits, *all* of the information used by a computer is represented. The value of a bit is easily implemented electronically in terms of a circuit that is either on (1) or off (0). The values of bits can be transmitted electronically in terms of pulses of electrical signals, a strong pulse representing 1, and a weak pulse representing 0.

15 Beringia (bə-rĭn′jē-ə)

The region of land between the Kolyma River in eastern Russia and the Mackenzie River in the Northwest Territories of Canada, now separated by the Bering Strait.

The term *Beringia* is mostly used to describe the region during periods of low water level, especially during the last ice age (between 22,000 and 7,000 years ago), when it constituted a land bridge now known as the Bering Land Bridge. During this period, the first humans to migrate to North America, peoples who were in all likelihood the ancestors of most or all Native Americans, are thought to have made their way through the region from Asia. Beringia itself was not covered with ice during this period, and many plants and other animals, including a now extinct species of lion, also found their way from Asia to America.

[After Vitus *Bering* (1681–1741), Danish explorer who in 1728 sailed through the Bering Strait, proving (though he did not realize it at the time) that Asia and North America are separate continents.]

16 big bang

The explosion of an extremely small, hot, and dense body of matter that, according to some cosmological theories, gave rise to the universe between 12 and 20 billion years ago.

According to the widely accepted theory of the big bang, the universe was originally smaller than a dime and almost infinitely dense. A massive explosion, which kicked off the expansion, was the origin of all known space, matter, energy, and time. In the 1920s astronomer Edwin Hubble discovered that wherever one looked in space, distant galaxies were rapidly moving away from the earth, and the more distant the galaxy the greater its speed. Through this observation he determined that the universe was becoming larger. Hubble also found that the ratio between a galaxy's distance and velocity (speed and direction of travel) was constant. This value, called the *Hubble constant,* indicates the rate at which the universe is expanding. By calculating the distance and velocity of various galaxies and working backward, astronomers could determine how long ago the expansion began — in other words, the age of the universe. This figure, which scientists are constantly refining, is currently thought to be between 12 and 20 billion years.

DARKNESS VISIBLE

How can we see an object so perfectly dark that no light can escape from anywhere near it? We cannot see it directly, but astronomers do sometimes find stars that appear to be orbiting around some unseen companion: a good candidate for a **black hole.** In some cases, the force of the black hole's gravity sucks in gaseous material from an orbiting star, and this material forms a spinning disk as it spirals into the black hole, becoming so hot that it emits large amounts of powerful x-rays before entering the event horizon. This radiation can be detected, making black holes quite visible after all.

17 black hole

An extremely dense celestial object whose gravitational field is so strong that not even light can escape from its vicinity.

Black holes are believed to form in the aftermath of a *supernova*—the catastrophic explosion of large stars—with the collapse of the star's core. If there is enough mass in this collapsed star, it becomes a black hole. Black holes are extremely dense: for the sun, which has a diameter of about 1,390,000 kilometers (862,000 miles), to be as dense as a black hole, its entire mass would have to be squeezed down to a ball fewer than 5 kilometers (3 miles) across. Some theorists believe that the material in a black hole is compressed to a single point of infinite density called a *singularity*. Black holes are thought to reside in the centers of many galaxies, including our own Milky Way.

18 Brownian motion

The random movement of microscopic particles suspended in a liquid or gas, caused by collisions between these particles and the molecules of the liquid or gas.

In the early 19th century, the Scottish botanist Robert Brown noticed that very small pieces of pollen, floating in water and observed under a microscope, underwent constant random motion. That this motion was not due to the pollen's being alive was quickly ascertained by noting that pieces of dust also moved in this way.

Remarkably enough, these observations turned out to be of great importance to the development of atomic and molecular theory, as well as to theories of stock-market prices. In 1900, French mathematician Louis Bachelier published a theory of the motion, explaining it as the cumulative result of small impacts on the pollen and dust from random directions. Bachelier used this mathematical model to understand random fluctuations in stock-market prices.

Five years later, Albert Einstein (unaware of Bachelier's work) developed a similar theory. He pointed out that the *kinetic theory* of fluids, the then still controversial theory that fluids were made of large numbers of tiny moving pieces (atoms or molecules), predicted precisely such motion. The atoms or molecules, bouncing randomly against the pollen or dust, would push it this way and that. Einstein's analysis of Brownian motion supported the kinetic theory of fluids.

19

Cambrian Explosion
(kăm′brē-ən *or* kām′brē-ən)

The apparent rapid diversification of multicellular animal life that took place around the beginning of the Cambrian Period (540 to 505 million years ago), when the earth was characterized by warm seas and desert land areas.

During the Cambrian Explosion, almost all modern animal phyla (major classification groups) begin to appear in the fossil record. The first traces of mollusks, arthropods, echinoderms, and chordates (the group that includes vertebrates like humans) all date from the Cambrian. This sudden appearance of many animal phyla in the fossil record has sparked considerable debate among scientists about the rate at which evolution proceeds. Some have argued that it can proceed by leaps and jumps, with periods of extremely rapid evolution, while others argue that the sudden appearance of diversity in the Cambrian period is an illusion, because it is possible that conditions were not favorable for the formation of fossils before the Cambrian. In fact, evidence from DNA suggests that most of the animal phyla had appeared long before the Cambrian Period.

[From Medieval Latin *Cambria,* Wales (where rocks from this period were first found), alteration of *Cumbria,* from Welsh *Cymry,* from British Celtic **kom-brogos,* countryman, from Proto-Indo-European **kom,* with, beside + **merg-,* boundary, border (also the source of English *mark,* from Old English *mearc,* landmark).]

CAMBRIAN FOSSILS

Some of the animals of the **Cambrian Explosion** sported bizarre combinations of legs, spines, segments, and heads found in no present-day animals. A great deal of our knowledge about these early animals comes from the Burgess Shale, a 540-million-year-old formation of black shale discovered in 1909 by Charles Walcott in the Rocky Mountains of British Columbia. The rare process of fossilization that occurred in the Burgess Shale allowed exquisite preservation of Cambrian life forms. Bacteria and other organisms that require oxygen usually decompose soft animal parts before they can be fossilized, but the Burgess Shale animals lived deep in the ocean, where there is limited oxygen. They were buried by a mudslide, and the lack of oxygen prevented their decay. The mud then hardened into shale, preserving the soft animal parts.

At the time of his discovery, Walcott was able to classify the fossils as ancestors of modern animals. The Burgess Shale was reexamined in the mid-1960s, and many new, unknown fossils were found. When Harry Whittington, Derek Briggs, and Simon Conway Morris studied these new fossils in the 1970s and 1980s, they realized that many of them did not fit into the modern classification system. Debate has raged about the interpretation of fossils from the Cambrian ever since.

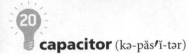

capacitor (kə-păs′ĭ-tər)

*An electrical device consisting of two conducting plates sepa-
rated by an electrical insulator called a* dielectric *and designed
to hold an electric charge.*

Charge builds up in a capacitor when a voltage is applied
across the plates, creating an electric field between them.
Different dielectric materials and the size of and distance between the two plates affect how much charge can be held.

The capacity to hold an electric charge makes the capacitor a bit like a small battery. The buildup of charge "stores"
power at the voltage that was applied to it. This is useful for
keeping a small amount of power available in devices that
have been unplugged from a power source, and is also the
reason that electrical devices that use high voltages, such as
televisions, can be dangerous even when unplugged: the capacitors inside them can retain hundreds of volts for days or
weeks, with enough power to cause serious injury.

Though capacitors resist the flow of direct current, the

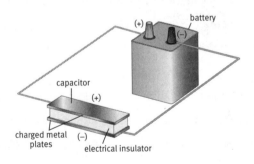

CAPACITOR

A capacitor is charged when electrons from a power source, such as a
battery, flow to one of the two plates. Because the electrons cannot
pass through the insulating layer, they build up on the first plate, giving
it a negative charge. Electrons on the other plate are drawn toward the
positive terminal of the battery, causing that plate to become positively
charged. An electric field develops between the two plates.

---

capacitor / carbon sequestration 22

charge-carrying capacity of a capacitor allows it to create currents if the voltage across it is *changing*. This makes capacitors useful in passing (or shunting off) alternating currents, a property with a huge number of uses, especially in manipulating signals processed in amplifiers, radios, and computers.

21 carbon sequestration

The long-term removal of carbon dioxide (the principle gas that traps heat from the sun) from the atmosphere, especially when considered as a mechanism that can prevent or reduce global warming.

Some scientists propose that the effects of global warming can be lessened by allowing living organisms to *sequester* carbon dioxide from the atmosphere and store it in their own bodies. Forests can act as *carbon sinks* when the trees in the forest absorb more carbon dioxide while making carbohydrates through photosynthesis than they release as waste from processes of growth and maintenance. The carbon removed from the atmosphere is then stored in the form of wood, which is made up of complex carbohydrates like cellulose. The ongoing destruction of forests, peat bogs, and other environments that can store large amounts of carbon may thus worsen the effects of global warming.

[**CARBON:** From French *carbone,* from Latin *carbō, carbōn-,* a coal, charcoal, from Proto-Indo-European **ker-,* heat, fire (also the source of English *cremate* and *ceramic*). **SEQUESTRATION:** Ultimately from Latin *sequestrāre,* to give up for safekeeping, from Latin *sequester,* depositary, trustee, from Proto-Indo-European **sek^w-,* to follow (also the source of English *second* and *social*).]

centripetal force (sĕn-trĭp′ĭ-tl)

A force acting on a moving body at an angle to the direction of motion, tending to make the body follow a circular or curved path.

Objects in motion tend to travel in a straight line at constant speed unless acted on by an external force. To make an object travel along a curved path, some force—the centripetal force—must push the body toward the *center of curvature* of that path. In the case of a circular path, the direction of the force is toward the center of rotation.

The earth's gravity acts as a centripetal force on orbiting objects, such as the earth's moon, which is constantly being accelerated toward the center of the earth. The moon has enough inertia not to plummet into the earth, but not so much that it can escape the earth's pull, and thus it will orbit almost indefinitely. The friction of the tires of a car making a turn similarly provides centripetal force on the car, causing it to turn, and the car's seats and walls exert a centripetal force on the passengers, causing them to follow the path along with the car.

Centripetal force is sometimes confused with *centrifugal force,* which is not a real force, but the effect of an object's inertia when that object is pushed by some other object with a centripetal force—the feeling of being pushed to the side in a turning car, for an example.

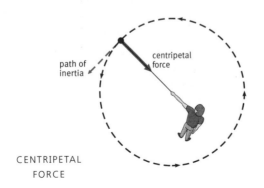

path of inertia

centripetal force

CENTRIPETAL FORCE

chemosynthesis (kē′mō-sĭn′thĭ-sĭs)

The production of food (carbohydrates) by an organism using the energy released from chemical reactions instead of the energy of sunlight.

As recently as the 1970s, scientists thought that almost all life ultimately depended on photosynthesis carried on by plants, algae, and certain bacteria. The deep sea was almost completely unexplored at the time, and it seemed that life on the ocean floor survived on the "rain" of organic material from above and was thus dependent on photosynthesis at or near the surface as well. But then deep-sea explorers discovered that rich, varied communities of organisms were living near deep-sea vents — openings in the ocean floor that spew hot water rich in inorganic compounds. Microorganisms living in these ecosystems produce their food by using energy derived from chemical reactions involving the inorganic compounds released from the vents. Other members of the deep-sea vent community then feed on the chemosynthetic microorganisms, and some house the microorganisms in their own bodies in a symbiotic relationship. Certain cave environments also harbor ecosystems dependent on chemosynthetic organisms.

[**CHEMO-:** Ultimately from New Latin *chimicus,* alchemist, from Medieval Latin *alchimicus,* from *alchymia,* alchemy, from Arabic *al-kīmiyā':* al-, the + *kīmiyā',* chemistry (from Late Greek *khēmeia, khumeia,* perhaps from Greek *Khēmia,* Egypt). **SYNTHESIS:** Ultimately from Greek *sunthesis,* collection, from *suntithenai,* to put together, from *sun,* with + *tithenai,* to put (from Proto-Indo-European **dhē-,* also the source of Modern English *deed* and *do*).]

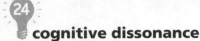

cognitive dissonance

(kŏg′nĭ-tĭv dĭs′ə-nəns)

The psychological tension that occurs when one holds mutually exclusive beliefs or attitudes and that often motivates people to modify their thoughts or behaviors in order to reduce the tension.

People are usually comfortable with what they know or believe to be true, but new information can contradict these beliefs. When confronted with these contradictions, people must change either their thinking or their behavior in order to reduce the resulting psychological conflict. A good example of this is when a person who enjoys smoking reads an article describing the damaging effects of cigarettes on the body. Because this new information makes smoking seem dangerous and foolish, it conflicts with the person's preexisting feeling that smoking is an enjoyable and worthy pursuit. Living with this disturbing feeling is difficult and unpleasant. To reduce the tension, the smoker must either quit smoking or reject the idea that smoking actually damages health.

Research in cognitive dissonance has provided explanations for behaviors that are counterintuitive or apparently irrational. For example, early research on cognitive dissonance noted that members of groups who undergo initiations tended to place a higher value on belonging to a group when the initiation was more uncomfortable or humiliating, as in the case of hazing. This seeming contradiction made sense, however, when it was shown that placing a low value on group membership would create too much cognitive dissonance for initiates who had paid a high price to become members.

complementarity (kŏm′plə-měn-tăr′ĭ-tē)

The concept that the underlying properties of entities (especially subatomic particles) may manifest themselves in mutually exclusive forms at different times, depending on the conditions of observation, and that any physical model that describes entities in terms of one form or the other will be incomplete.

Complementarity is the result of a remarkable episode in scientific history: the development of quantum mechanics. Complementarity was needed to explain what at first appeared to be contradictory observations.

Take light, for instance. Physicists have observed that light comes in discrete units, ricochets off mirrors, and carries momentum. This suggests that light is made of small particles. Yet under some conditions, light appears to act like a wave, having an observable wavelength and polarization, causing interference patterns, bending around corners, and so on. This combination of properties is known as *wave-particle duality*. Depending on the conditions of observation, particle theories or wave theories explain the behavior of light extremely well, and yet the human imagination cannot conceive of an entity that is both a particle and a wave, and so scientists had no way of unifying the two theories.

To develop a new theory that explained the behavior of light under any condition, scientists needed to let go of the idea that light must really be either a particle or a wave, and accept the principle of complementarity. Eventually a unified quantum mechanical understanding of light was developed in a theory called *quantum electrodynamics,* one of the most successful scientific theories of all time. Nonetheless, the principle of complementarity still retains, even among physicists, a sense of the mysterious.

[Ultimately from Latin *complēmentum*, something that completes, from *complēre*, to fill out, from *com-*, intensive prefix + *plēre*, to fill (from Proto-Indo-European *pelə-*, to fill, also the source of English *full* and *fill*).]

A SECRET HANDSHAKE

How do two parties agree on a keyword to use for encryption? If they don't have a secure communication channel, a snooper could catch wind of the keyword — but if they do, they don't need encryption to start with! This age-old problem was solved after World War II with the development of *public key* **cryptography,** in which *two* keywords are used: one of them, the *public key*, encrypts the message in such a way that only the other, the *private key*, can decrypt it. The online store sends its public key to the customer, whose computer encrypts his or her personal information with it. The ciphertext thus created can now be safely transmitted, since only the online store, which keeps the crucial private key to itself, can decrypt it.

26 cryptography (krĭp-tŏg′rə-fē)

The rendering of information into a form that cannot be read or understood without the knowledge of some secret method or key.

Sending messages in coded form has a long history in warfare, espionage, and romance. But the rise of computer and telecommunications technology has made cryptography an everyday, though mostly invisible, affair. When a buyer purchases a product from an online store on the Internet with a credit card, for example, the card number, along with other personal information, is usually *encrypted* into a form called a *ciphertext.* This ciphertext, rather than the original information or *plaintext,* is what is transmitted, since it can be read only by being decrypted by the intended recipient, and not by anyone snooping in on the transmission.

This kind of encryption and decryption uses what is called a *cipher.* Cyphers are algorithms that rely on special numbers called *keys.* Keys are in effect the passwords needed to encrypt and decrypt the information.

[Ultimately from Greek *kruptos,* hidden + *graphiā,* writing (from *graphein,* to write, from Proto-Indo-European *gerbh-,* to scratch, also the source of English *carve*).]

cyanobacterium (sī'ə-nō-băk-tîr'ē-əm)
Plural: **cyanobacteria** (sī'ə-nō-băk-tîr'ē-ə)

A photosynthetic bacterium of the class Coccogoneae or Hormogoneae, generally blue-green in color and in some species capable of nitrogen fixation.

Among the earliest known life forms, cyanobacteria appear in fossils that are 2.7 billion years old and exist today in some 7,500 species. Cyanobacteria can occur as individual cells or as multicellular filaments. Common colonial species secrete a mucilaginous substance that binds the cells or filaments together in colored masses. Many organisms, especially plants, have symbiotic relationships with cyanobacteria and benefit from their ability to photosynthesize or to fix nitrogen. And all life benefits from the oxygen cyanobacteria release as a byproduct of metabolism. In fact, much of the earth's atmospheric oxygen is thought to have been produced by cyanobacteria.

Cyanobacteria are sometimes called *blue-green algae,* but they differ from most algae in that they are *prokaryotic.* That is, cyanobacteria lack the membrane-bound organelles, such as nuclei or mitochondria, that are found within *eukaryotic* cells. Cyanobacteria conduct photosynthesis in invaginations of the cell membrane called *thylakoids.* Since thylakoids also occur in the photosynthetic organelles called *chloroplasts* (the structures that conduct photosynthesis in plants and algae), scientists speculate that chloroplasts were originally free-floating cyanobacteria that were incorporated into the cells of other organisms in a kind of symbiosis.

[**CYANO-:** From Greek *kuano-,* from *kuanos,* dark blue. **BACTERIUM:** From New Latin *bactērium,* from Greek *baktērion,* diminutive of *baktron,* rod, from Proto-Indo-European *bak-,* staff used for support (also the source of Modern English *peg*).]

28
cyclone

An atmospheric region of low air pressure around which air flows in an inward spiral. In the Northern Hemisphere the air moves counterclockwise around the low-pressure center, and in the Southern Hemisphere the air travels clockwise.

The companion term *anticyclone* refers to a region of high air pressure around which air flows in an outward spiral. The air moves in the opposite direction from that of a cyclone. The words *cyclonic* and *anticyclonic* are also used to describe just the direction of motion. For example, tornadoes are a kind of cyclone, and in the Northern Hemisphere they typically involve counterclockwise air flow. However, tornadoes occasionally form with anticyclonic winds, flowing clockwise into the low-pressure center of the tornado.

Tropical cyclones are large weather systems that develop over warm water. Severe tropical cyclones, with winds of 119 kilometers (74 miles) per hour or greater, are better known as *hurricanes* when they occur in the Atlantic Ocean and Gulf of Mexico, or as *typhoons* when they happen in the Pacific Ocean.

Because the word *cyclone* broadly defines a kind of atmospheric flow, cyclones are not confined to our planet. In 1999, the Hubble Space Telescope photographed a cyclone more than 1,610 kilometers (1,000 miles) across in the northern polar regions of Mars.

[From Greek *kuklōn*, present participle of *kukloun*, to rotate, from *kuklos*, circle, from Proto-Indo-European *k^wel-*, to turn (also the source of English *wheel*).]

29. dendrochronology (děn′drō-krə-nŏl′ə-jē)

The study of growth rings in trees for the purpose of analyzing past climate conditions or determining the dates of past events.

A growth ring is a layer of wood formed in a tree during a single period of growth. Because trees grow more slowly in periods of drought or other environmental stress than they do under more favorable conditions, the size of the rings they produce varies. When a tree is cut crosswise, the growth rings are visible as concentric circles of varying width, and analyzing the pattern of a tree's rings provides information about the environmental changes that took place during the period in which it was growing. Matching the pattern in trees whose age is known to the pattern in wood or charcoal found at an archaeological site can establish the date at which the wood was cut and thus the approximate date of the site as well. Some pieces of wood or charcoal may include not only rings that can be matched with those of the oldest living trees in the region but also rings that are even older. These can be used to extend the dendrochronological record into the past beyond the age of the oldest living trees. By comparing living trees with old lumber and finding overlapping ring patterns, scientists have established chronological records for some species and regions that go back as far as 9,000 years.

[**DENDRO-:** From Greek *dendron*, tree, from Proto-Indo-European **deru-*, **dreu-*, wood (also the source of Modern English *tree*).
CHRONOLOGY: From New Latin *chronologia*, ultimately from Greek *khronos*, time + *-logia*, discourse (from *logos*, word, speech).]

echolocation (ĕk′ō-lō-kā′shən)

A sensory system, such as that found in bats and dolphins, in which usually high-pitched sounds are emitted and their echoes interpreted to determine the position, speed, shape, and texture of objects in the environment.

Echolocation is found among animals that are nocturnal or that live in environments with very little light. Insectivorous bats, or microbats, are particularly adept at echolocation— they can recognize and pinpoint flying objects as small as gnats or mosquitoes, typical prey insects for some species. Echolocation is also used by the toothed whales (the group including dolphins and killer whales), a few cave-dwelling bird species, and perhaps also some seals. Certain shrews and tenrecs (a diverse family of mammals with many species in Madagascar) use a rudimentary form of echolocation.

Both dolphins and bats echolocate using sounds with frequencies ranging up to 200,000 hertz. In contrast, humans can hear sounds only up to about 20,000 hertz at best. Microbats produce the sounds used in echolocation in their larynx, the same organ that humans use to produce many speech sounds and to sing. The sounds may be amplified and focused by the nose-leaf, the leaflike folds of tissue on the face of a microbat that give some species a grotesque appearance—at least by human standards. Dolphins and other toothed whales, on the other hand, produce their echolocative sounds with specialized flaplike organs located within their head near the opening of their blowhole.

Echolocation is also found in humans. Some blind people are able to navigate in physically complex spaces such as forests or city streets by listening to the echoes of clicks, made either with the tongue or by a special device.

[ECHO: From Middle English, from Old French, from Latin *ēchō*, from Greek *ēkhō*, from Proto-Indo-European *swāg-*, to resound (also the source of Old English *swōgan*, Modern English *sough*). LOCATION: From Latin *locatio, locatiōn-*, a placing, from *locāre*, to place, from *locus*, place.]

NEEDLES THAT STOP PAIN

Acupuncture needles inserted at certain body locations have been found to successfully treat some chronic pain conditions such as arthritis and back pain and to induce anesthesia. The needles are believed to stimulate the production of **endorphins**. Laboratory experiments show that when acupuncture subjects are given drugs that interfere with the attachment of endorphins to their receptors, the acupuncture treatment fails to relieve pain. Exactly how acupuncture stimulates endorphin production is not understood.

31

endorphin (ĕn-dôr′fĭn)

A substance that is secreted mainly in the brain and inhibits the perception of pain.

Endorphins are long chains of amino acids, known as *polypeptides,* that are able to bind to specific molecules called *receptors* in the nervous system and relieve pain in a way similar to that of morphine. They were discovered in the 1970s when scientists were investigating why opiate drugs like morphine and heroin were such effective painkillers. Researchers concluded that opiate receptors probably exist because the body produces endogenous morphine-like compounds, or endorphins, that also bind to the specialized receptors. Endorphins were ultimately isolated from the pituitary gland.

Of the three major types of endorphins, *beta-endorphins* are found almost entirely in the pituitary gland, while *enkephalins* and *dynorphins* are distributed throughout the nervous system. Besides behaving as *analgesics,* or pain reducers, endorphins are thought to modulate the appetite, cause the release of sex hormones, and bring on euphoric feelings. Prolonged, continuous exercise such as running, for example, causes an increased production of endorphins, resulting in the so-called "runner's high."

[Blend of *endo*(*genous*) and (*mo*)*rphin*(*e*). *Morphine,* from *Morpheus,* the god of dreams in Ovid's *Metamorphoses,* from Greek *morphē,* form, shape.]

32 estivation (ĕs'tə-vā'shən)

A state of being dormant during the summer.

Everyone knows that certain animals hibernate in the winter, but some species actually prefer to take the summer off. These animals enter an inactive state called *estivation,* a torpor resembling deep sleep that protects them from heat, dryness, and sunlight during the hot summer months. Like hibernation, estivation is a method of conserving bodily energy and water by decreasing metabolic functions during a time of environmental stress. Estivating animals don't usually eat, move, or grow.

Animals that estivate include desert-dwelling squirrels, frogs, toads, bees, and salamanders. Many burrow underground. Some frogs surround themselves in a layer of molted skin to protect themselves from drought. Lungfish, elongated freshwater fishes of the Amazon, western and central Africa, and Australia, have lunglike organs as well as gills and are able to breathe air. This allows them to estivate in the mud inside mucus-lined cocoons, which are secreted from their own bodies and harden into thick cysts. Some species such as earthworms, snakes, and snails both estivate and hibernate. Snails attach themselves to walls or trees. After pulling into their shells, a secreted substance seals off the external environment to keep in moisture.

[From Latin *aestās,* summer.]

33

eutrophication (yōō-trŏf′ĭ-kā′shən)

The process by which the water in an aquatic ecosystem, such as a lake, stream, or estuary, becomes rich in nutrients that promote a proliferation of plant life and algae.

Some aquatic environments undergo eutrophication as a natural process. In the water of a young lake left by the melting of a glacier, for example, there may be few nutrients like nitrogen and phosphorus available to plants and algae. The lake will support relatively little life despite an abundance of oxygen in the waters. As minerals and organic material run off the land into the lake, the increased availability of nutrients allows plants and algae to thrive, which in turn leads to a greater number and diversity of organisms that feed on them. Gradually, the lake is filled in by the accumulation of organic materials until it becomes a wetland. At all stages in such natural processes of eutrophication, there is a diverse set of organisms appropriate to the ecological conditions.

Human activities, however, often add a large amount of nutrients to bodies of water, as when agricultural fertilizers run off fields and animal and human waste is discharged. This sudden availability of nutrients triggers blooms of algae, especially cyanobacteria. When the algae die, they are consumed by bacteria that use up the oxygen in water as part of the process of decay. The dense growth of algae also prevents light from reaching aquatic plants that provide food and shelter for a diverse range of species. As a result, many organisms in the ecosystem die, and there is a great loss of biodiversity. The fish in the ecosystem, for example, may be asphyxiated or starve to death. Such anthropogenic (human-caused) eutrophication of lakes, estuaries, and other bodies of water is one of the most serious ecological problems facing the world today.

[From Greek *eutrophos*, well-nourished : *eu-*, good, well + *trephein*, to nourish.]

Fibonacci sequence (fē′bə-nä′chē)

A sequence of numbers beginning with two arbitrary numbers, such that each following number is equal to the sum of the two preceding numbers.

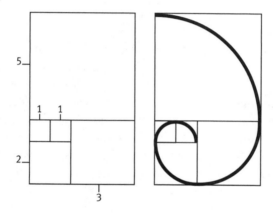

FIBONACCI SEQUENCE

The sequence 0, 1, 1, 2, 3, 5, 8, 13, 21, 34, 55 . . . is a Fibonacci sequence. A *Fibonacci number* is any of the numbers from the infinite Fibonacci sequence beginning with 0 and 1, as in the sequence above.

The idea behind the Fibonacci sequence is very simple. It is named after an Italian mathematician, also known as Leonardo of Pisa, who conceived the sequence as a simple, rough way of modeling the growth of a population of rabbits, although the sequence had been investigated as early as the 12th century in India. The sequence does appear quite often in the natural world, especially in the growth of plants, for example in the number and arrangement of seeds in the spiral structures of raspberries and sunflowers, or the increasing size of the spiral shape of a nautilus shell.

The ratio between successive Fibonacci numbers narrows in on a particular value as the sequence progresses. This limit value is known as the *Golden Ratio* or *Golden Mean,* equal to $(\sqrt{5}-1) / 2$. Objects with proportions in this ratio are considered especially pleasing to the eye. Ancient Greek architecture made much use of this proportion.

[After Leonardo *Fibonacci* (died circa 1250), Italian mathematician.]

fission (fĭsh′ən *or* fĭzh′ən)

1. *The splitting of an unstable atomic nucleus into two or more nuclei, usually resulting in the release of energy in the form of electromagnetic radiation and fast-moving subatomic particles.*

Fission occurs spontaneously when a large, heavy nucleus, such as that of a uranium atom, has an excess of neutrons. An atom of uranium-235, for example, is fairly stable, but if it absorbs a neutron, it becomes unstable and will almost immediately split into several smaller pieces, each of which has a great deal of kinetic energy, and will release a large amount of electromagnetic radiation as well. But some of these pieces are themselves neutrons, and others are radioactive and will soon emit neutrons. If there is another uranium-235 atom in the vicinity, it might absorb one of these neutrons and undergo fission itself. This means that fission can induce a chain reaction, given a sufficient quantity of uranium. Such chain reactions are the principle behind the atomic bomb. Nuclear reactors exploit the same kinds of fission reactions but control the reaction by regulating the speed and number of neutrons, preventing too many of them from inducing fission.

2. *A process of asexual reproduction in which a single cell splits to form two identical, independent cells.*

In fission, the chromosomal DNA replicates before the cell divides. Most bacteria and other prokaryotes reproduce by means of fission.

[From Latin *fissiō, fissiōn-*, a cleaving, from *fissus*, past participle of *findere*, to split, from Proto-Indo-European *bheid-*, to split (also the source of English *bite*).]

FISSION

three nuclei of uranium-235 undergoing fission in a chain reaction

36 fundamental force

Any one of the forces that act between bodies of matter. The four known fundamental forces are the electromagnetic force, *the* strong force, gravity, *and the* weak force.

All electromagnetic radiation, including ordinary light, is nothing more than the way objects with electrical charge interact with each other: when we see the color of an apple, the electrons on the surface of the apple are exerting a force on the electrons in our eyes. *Photons,* the particles associated with light, are said in physics to *carry* or *mediate* this force, the electromagnetic force.

The strong force is a short-range but powerful attractive force. It bundles the elementary particles called *quarks* together into larger particles such as protons and neutrons, and bundles protons and neutrons together into atomic nuclei. It has a set of mediating particles called *gluons.* Quarks are constantly exchanging gluons. In fact, nearly half the momentum of a proton is in its gluons.

Some theories of gravity posit the existence of a mediating particle called a *graviton,* but this particle has never been observed. It would presumably be what carries the force of attraction between two bodies.

The weak force is responsible for the phenomenon of radioactive decay. It has three mediating particles, the W^+, W^-, and Z^0 bosons, which mediate interactions between quarks and other particles called *leptons,* such as electrons. A theory of the *electroweak force* explains electromagnetism and the weak force as two manifestations of a single underlying force. Physicists hope eventually to explain all of the fundamental forces as different manifestations of a single underlying force or physical principle.

37 game theory

The mathematical modeling of competitive situations, used to determine optimal courses of action for an interested partici-

pant, and to model the dynamics of competitive situations and the behavior of their participants.

We generally think of games as ways to amuse ourselves during leisure time, but games of all kinds are also the subject of serious mathematical study. The rules of many games can be understood as a sort of mathematical system, and the various consequences of different behavior by the players can be studied. But game theory is actually applied much more broadly, for example in political, economic, and military planning; economic theory, in particular, has benefited from game-theory approaches.

38

genome (jē'nōm')

All the genetic information in the chromosomes of an organism, including its genes and other DNA sequences.

DNA is largely made up of a string of molecules linked together in pairs known as *base pairs*. Some sequences of base pairs form *genes*, which guide growth and development by telling cells how to build particular proteins. The Human Genome Project, a worldwide research effort that took place between 1990 and 2003, identified and discovered the exact sequence of the approximately 3 billion base pairs that make up the human genome. In comparison, viruses contain only thousands of base pairs, and some plants have more than 100 billion.

The project identified almost 20,000 human genes. Researchers estimate that there may be up to 5,000 more genes left to identify. This is a lower total number of human genes than had previously been predicted. In fact, some other organisms have many more genes than humans do. For example, the genome of rice plants contains about 50,000 genes. Once all of the human genes have been identified, there will still be much more work to do; researchers know the actual biological function of only about half the genes that have been identified.

gluon (gloo′ŏn)

The subatomic particle that mediates the strong force, one of the four fundamental forces of nature.

Gluons are similar to photons, the carriers of the electromagnetic force (and thus of electromagnetic radiation, like light or x-rays). When two particles that have an electric charge, such as two electrons or an electron and a proton, interact with each other, they exchange photons. Similarly, gluons are exchanged between particles, most notably quarks, that have a property known as *color charge.*

The protons and neutrons that form the nuclei of all atoms are made of quarks. The strong force holds the quarks together, and it acts like a rubber band: as long as the quarks are very close, they are very free to move around (the rubber band is loose, so to speak), but the farther away the quarks get from each other, the greater the pull back together. The constant exchange of gluons in a proton or neutron is analogous to these rubber bands, resulting in a force so strong that it is thought to be impossible for quarks to exist in isolation (and indeed, no quarks have ever been observed in isolation).

Like photons, gluons have no mass of their own, but they nonetheless carry momentum. In fact, nearly half of the momentum of a proton or neutron is attributable to the massless gluons holding them together. Unlike photons, which themselves have no electric charge and so pass through each other without effect, gluons have color charge and thus interact with each other. This entails that there may exist little bundles of matter made only of gluons. These particles are called *glueballs,* and particle physicists are actively looking for them in experiments.

[From *glue* (from Middle English *glu,* from Old French, from Late Latin *glūs,* from Latin *glūten,* from Proto-Indo-European **glei-,* clay, also the source of English *clay*) + *-on,* suffix used in the names of subatomic particles.]

40

heliocentrism (hē'lē-ō-sĕn'trĭz'əm)

A theory or model of the solar system or universe having the sun as the center.

Although modern astronomy no longer believes that the universe has any exact center, heliocentrism was a very important shift away from the notion of geocentrism, in which the earth was considered to be the center of the universe. It stood to reason that the earth was a fixed point around which the sun, moon, stars, and planets all revolved, since they appeared to do so in the sky, and people on the earth could feel no effects of motion. But the gradual motion of the planets in relation to the stars and to each other was difficult to fit into the picture. The heliocentric view, in particular the ideas advanced by Nicolaus Copernicus in the 16th century, provided a different interpretation of the motion of the planets that explained their motion more simply.

His heliocentric system was modeled after an earlier system developed by the Greek astronomer Ptolemy, in which the sun is at the center of the universe, with all the planets and stars revolving around it in circular orbits. This model of the universe was disputed by most astronomers of the time, and it appeared to many theologians to contradict certain Biblical passages; in fact, Copernicus's treatise on the subject was listed on the Catholic Church's Index of Forbidden Books from 1616 until 1835. However, theoretical support for Copernicus's system was provided by Sir Isaac Newton's theory of universal gravitation. The model of the solar system held by modern astronomers does not have planets in circular motion around the sun, but it is incontrovertibly heliocentric.

[Ultimately from Greek *hēlios,* sun (from Proto-Indo-European **sāwel-,* also the source of English *sun* and Latin *sōl,* sun, and *sōlāris,* solar) + Latin *centrum,* center (from Greek *kentron,* point of a spear, stationary point of pair of compasses, center of a circle, from *kentein,* to prick) + Greek *-ikos,* adjectival suffix.]

histone (hĭs′tōn′)

Any of several proteins that are bound to the DNA in most cells and play important roles in controlling how genes are expressed.

Organisms that have nuclei in their cells—that is, nearly all organisms except bacteria—have large amounts of DNA, and these DNA molecules are often huge. In humans they contain 3 billion base pairs, and some organisms have up to 100 billion. How does a cell store and organize all of this chemical information so that the cell functions as it should?

DNA is often pictured as a long, drawn-out spiral ladder, but when the cell is not replicating, the DNA in the nucleus is strung around a series of proteins known as *histones.* Their chief functions are to compact and control the long threads of DNA. They do this by interacting with each other to form a structure like a spool. Two hundred base pairs of DNA are wrapped in two turns around this spool, forming the subunits known as *nucleosomes,* and decreasing the effective length of DNA by a factor of eight. These DNA-histone complexes look like a series of beads on a string. In this way 20 million base pairs of DNA (a base pair is one of the "rungs" on the DNA ladder) can be organized into approximately 100,000 nucleosome core particles. The complexes are further compacted by a factor of four by a linker histone that binds the DNA between the nucleosomes, organizing them into a coil.

Histones are also one of the ways that cells control which sequences of DNA are turned on for transcription of RNA, the template for making the proteins necessary for the cell to function and reproduce. When histones are chemically modified in certain ways, they can loosen their hold on the DNA and allow it to become accessible to proteins that activate transcription, or they can tighten their hold on the DNA and make it inaccessible. This is one way that multicellular organisms can make multiple types of cells (such as muscle, liver, and skin), even though the different types of cells all contain the same DNA in their nuclei.

[German *Histon,* coined by German physician Albrecht Kossel (1853–1927), perhaps from New Latin *histo-,* bodily tissue (from Greek *histos,* loom, warp, piece of cloth, tissue) + German *-on,* suffix used to form names of organic compounds (equivalent to English suffix *-one*).]

hominin (hŏm′ə-nĭn)

A member of the biological group Hominini, characterized by such features as walking on two feet and including humans and their closest extinct relatives but not the other living species of great apes. The Hominini form a tribe (a degree of biological classification that is between a family and a genus) within the Hominidae, the family of the great apes.

As a result of recent extensive revisions of biological classification, many scientists now use the new term *hominin* to describe humans and their closest relatives and ancestors, the same group usually designated by the term *hominid* in the past. Older schemes of biological classification usually put humans and their close relatives in the family Hominidae (the hominids), while orangutans, gorillas, and chimpanzees were put in another family and separated completely from humans. In recent decades, however, scientists have tried to make biological classifications reflect the evolutionary history of organisms, and classifications have been revised on the basis of new genetic research as well. Such research has shown that chimps are more closely related to humans than they are to gorillas. Consequently, any classification that includes both gorillas and chimps should also include the nearest relatives of chimps—that is, humans.

To reflect these relationships, many scientists now classify all the great apes, including humans, in a single family, Hominidae (although schemes of classification remain in flux). Thus chimps, gorillas, and orangutans are now hominids along with humans. The term *hominin* is then used to distinguish modern humans and their extinct ancestors and relatives, like australopithecines and Neanderthals, from the other hominids, like chimps and gorillas.

[From Latin *homō, homin-,* man, human being, from Proto-Indo-European **dhghomō,* **dhghomon-,* earthling (as opposed to a god), human being, from **dhghem-,* earth.]

hypha (hī′fə)
Plural: **hyphae** (hī′fē)

One of the long slender tubes that form the structural parts of many fungi.

The fuzzy growth of mold on bread is composed of the growth of many hyphae. Mushrooms, the visible reproductive structures produced by some groups of fungi, are actually masses of densely packed hyphae. The form in which many fungi grow and take up food consists of a netlike mass of hyphae called a *mycelium,* although some fungi, such as yeasts, do not form hyphae.

The outer walls of hyphae are composed of chitin, the same substance that makes up the hard exoskeletons of insects. These walls form tubes that surround the cytoplasm, the jellylike material that makes up much of the inside of cells. However, hyphae are not divided into individual cells that resemble the cells of most animals and plants. Instead, many fungi, even quite large ones, consist of a single mass of cytoplasm distributed in a network of branching hyphae, and the nuclei of the fungi move freely within this mass. In some fungi, the hyphae have partitions called *septa* across which the cytoplasm flows.

[New Latin, from Greek *huphē*, web, from Proto-Indo-European *webh-, to weave (also the source of English *web, weave,* and *weft).*]

44

imaginary number

A number that is a multiple of i, *the square root of minus one.*

The notion that minus one has a square root seems at first to be a logical impossibility: every number on the number line, positive or negative, squares to a nonnegative number. But a shift in perspective can sometimes reveal new possibilities. The ancient Greeks, for example, thought all numbers were either whole numbers or ratios between them (fractions). Their discovery that some numbers, such as the square root of two, were not whole numbers or ratios was scandalous at the time. But once it was realized there was no need to restrict the concept of numbers this way, the problem disappeared; we now call such numbers *irrational numbers.*

IMAGINARY NUMBER

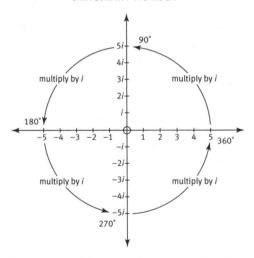

Multiplying the number 5 by the imaginary number *i* four times in succession "rotates" the number 5 back to its starting point.

In the case of *i*, the mistake is to look for it on the real number line. Imagine instead a second number line, perpendicular to the real number line and crossing it at zero (like the *y*-axis of a graph). If we stipulate that *i* is one unit up

---

imaginary number   **50**

from the intersection, $5i$ would be five units up, and so on. Multiplying a number on the real number line by i yields a number on the imaginary number line, and vice versa. For example, 5 multiplied by i gives $5i$—just as if 5 had been rotated 90 degrees counterclockwise to the imaginary number line. Multiplying $5i$ by i gives $5i^2$, which, since i is $\sqrt{-1}$, equals $5(-1)$, or -5, a *real* number—as if the original number, 5, had been swung underneath the real number line 180 degrees. Multiply *this* product by i—essentially a 270–degree rotation of 5—and we have $-5i$. One more multiplication completes the circle, yielding $-5i^2$, or $-5(-1)$, or 5, the number we started with. Thus i is a sort of number rotator that moves numbers out of and back into the real number line by 90 degrees each time.

This ability to model rotations makes imaginary numbers extremely useful. In fact, *complex numbers,* which are the sum of a real and an imaginary number, are badly named: many physics and engineering problems would be extremely difficult to solve without complex numbers.

45

interferon (ĭn′tər-fîr′ŏn′)

Any of a group of proteins that prevent viral replication in newly infected cells and promote immune functions in the body.

Interferons are glycoproteins (proteins joined to carbohydrates) produced by animal cells that have been infected or invaded by foreign agents such as viruses, bacteria, and tumors. The most important functions of these natural substances are to inhibit viruses and tumors and to regulate the body's immune system. Interferons inhibit viral replication and growth by interfering with the synthesis of viral proteins and preventing the entry of viruses into uninfected cells. They also inhibit the proliferation of tumor cells as well as the expression of genes that promote cancerous changes (known as *oncogenes*). In addition, interferons help to regulate and boost the immune system by promoting the activity of white blood cells such as lymphocytes, which kill viruses and infected cells.

Because of these properties, interferons are an effective treatment for certain infections, cancers, and autoimmune diseases. Although interferons are present in very small quantities in the body and are expensive to extract, recombinant DNA technology that became available in the early 1980s has made widespread production possible. Two types are particularly useful in clinical medicine and are manufactured as drugs. *Alpha interferon* is used to treat chronic hepatitis types B and C and several kinds of cancer, including leukemia and Kaposi's sarcoma, which is associated with AIDS. *Beta interferon* is used primarily in the treatment of multiple sclerosis.

[From *interfer(e)* + *-on,* suffix used in the names of chemical compounds.]

46

ischemia (ĭ-skē′mē-ə)

A decrease in the blood supply to a part of the body caused by constriction or obstruction of the blood vessels.

When a person has chest pain caused by ischemia, a condition called *angina,* it is usually the result of an obstructing blood clot or constricting spasm of the *coronary arteries,* the vessels that surround the heart and supply it with blood. The subsequent lack of oxygen sometimes causes the death of heart tissue, or a heart attack. Similarly, the obstruction or constriction of important neck arteries that supply the brain, called the *carotid arteries,* can cause ischemia of brain tissue, resulting in symptoms such as numbness or a stroke (the death of brain tissue). Smoking, high blood pressure, elevated blood cholesterol, and diabetes are major risk factors for ischemia.

[From Greek *iskhaimos,* a stopping of the blood : *iskhein*, to keep back + *haima*, blood.]

47 isomer (ī′sə-mər)

Any of two or more chemical compounds composed of the same elements in the same proportions and held together by the same type and number of chemical bonds but differing in structure.

Isomers that are very different in structure, such as two different proteins made of the same kinds and proportions of amino acids, usually behave differently in chemical interactions. But even isomers with a very similar structure can behave quite differently. Two isomers of propanol act like forms of alcohol, for example, while a third isomer is considered a kind of ether rather than alcohol.

Stereoisomers are isomers in which each atom in each isomer is bound to the same atoms as in the other isomers, but in a different spatial arrangement. A particularly interesting kind of stereoisomer is the *enantiomer*. Enantiomers come in pairs, such that each enantiomer is a mirror image of the other. They can be thought of as left-handed and right-handed versions of the same molecule. (In fact, the names of the enantiomers are often prefixed by *L*- and *R*-.) Much of our biochemistry is reliant on one or the other enantiomer of various compounds. For example, the chemical L-dopa can be used in the treatment of Parkinson's disease, but the enantiomer R-dopa is ineffective.

[From Greek *īsomerēs*, having equal share : *īsos,* alike, equal + *meros*, part, share (from Proto-Indo-European *(s)mer-, to get a share, also the source of English *merit,* from Latin *merēre, merērī,* to deserve, obtain).]

junk DNA

DNA that serves no known biological purpose (as in providing instructions for building proteins or otherwise regulating the expression of genes).

Junk DNA makes up the vast majority of DNA in the cells of most plants and animals. It composes at least 95 percent of human DNA. The percentage of the total DNA of a species that is junk DNA also varies greatly among species, even closely related ones. These facts raise some important questions for genetic researchers. Why would species have evolved with so much nonfunctional DNA? Where would all this useless DNA have come from? Or does junk DNA actually have functions that remain unclear to us?

If junk DNA did in fact serve no purpose, random mutations in it would leave the organism unaffected, and the organism would likely survive and reproduce, passing the mutated junk DNA to its offspring. Over thousands and millions of years, the mutations would accumulate, so that the junk DNA of distantly related organisms should be very dissimilar. Yet certain regions of junk DNA are remarkably similar among some distantly related mammal species, species whose common ancestors probably lived around 200 million years ago, leaving plenty of time for the DNA to accumulate different mutations.

This suggests that at least some junk DNA is not junk after all.

49
krill
Plural: **krill**

Any of various species of shrimplike marine crustaceans of the order Euphausiacea, especially the Antarctic krill (Euphausia superba), *that are one of the principal food sources for baleen whales and many other marine animals.*

Krill species range in size from 1 to 15 centimeters (.5 to 5.5 inches) and are filter-feeders, eating mostly diatoms and algae as well as animals smaller than themselves. They thus form a vital link in the food chain between the oceanic organisms that make their own food through photosynthesis and the larger animals higher on the food chain, such as fish, penguins, seals, and whales, that ultimately depend on them. For instance, the blue whale, the largest animal that has ever lived, feeds almost exclusively on krill. Antarctic krill in particular are an important part of the food chain of the Antarctic Ocean. Like almost all krill species, Antarctic krill are bioluminescent—they have organs near their eyes and on their thorax and abdomen that produce a greenish light. They use these lights to recognize each other and stay within the huge luminous shoals in which they move about the ocean.

[Norwegian *kril*, young fry of fish.]

HUMANS OUTWEIGHED BY KRILL

When considered in terms of sheer biomass —total mass of all individuals of a species taken together—Antarctic **krill** are probably the most successful and abundant single species of animal on the earth. Although the population of this species fluctuates from year to year, some scientists estimate that there may be over 500 million tons of Antarctic krill in the ocean, or perhaps twice the total biomass of humans.

KT boundary

The transition between the rocks of the Cretaceous and Tertiary periods, corresponding to a mass extinction event occurring 65 million years ago and resulting in the loss of up to 75 percent of all species in both terrestrial and aquatic environments.

During the Cretaceous period (144 to 65 million years ago), dinosaurs were still the dominant terrestrial animals, although mammals had already appeared. Early birds had already evolved from one group of dinosaurs. But at the KT boundary, all other groups of dinosaurs, the animals who had dominated the earth for over 130 million years, became extinct. During the following Tertiary period (65 to 2 million years ago), however, mammals came to fill many of the ecological niches left vacant by the dinosaurs.

In rock formations around the world, the KT boundary is distinguished by a layer of clay rich in iridium, an element that is rare in the earth's crust but relatively abundant in asteroids. Some scientists have therefore proposed that the KT boundary is the result of the impact of a large asteroid. This impact would have raised a huge dust cloud, blotted out the sun for several years, and caused other environmental disruptions. In fact, traces of a crater formed about 65 million years ago by such an impact have been found in the Yucatán Peninsula and underneath the Gulf of Mexico. Other scientists have proposed that huge volcano eruptions in India at the same period may have contributed to the decline in species by producing acid rain and warming the earth by the release of carbon dioxide. Still others have objected that some major extinctions appear to begin already in the late Cretaceous, perhaps as the result of climatic changes unrelated to asteroid impacts or volcanism. The end of the age of dinosaurs may thus result from the interaction of several factors, rather than from a single catastrophic event.

KT stands for *Cretaceous-Tertiary.* Since geologists reserve the letter *C* as an abbreviation for the Cambrian period (540 to 505 million years ago), the letter *K* is used instead.

---

51 Kuiper belt (kī′pər)

A disk-shaped region in the outer solar system lying beyond the orbit of Neptune and containing thousands of small, icy celestial bodies, believed to be a reservoir for short-period comets (comets that make one complete orbit of the sun in less than 200 years).

The bodies populating this region are known as *Kuiper belt objects.* There are an estimated 70,000 such objects having diameters of more than 100 km (62 mi). Pluto, which is traditionally classed with the planets, together with its moon Charon, is found in this region and is thought by some astronomers to be a large Kuiper belt object.

The Kuiper belt is named after American astronomer Gerard Kuiper (1905–1973), who first hypothesized its existence.

52 kwashiorkor (kwä′shē-ôr′kôr′)

A severe protein malnutrition, seen especially in infants and young children in developing nations after they are weaned.

Kwashiorkor is caused by a deficiency in the quality and quantity of protein in the diet. It is characterized by growth retardation, lethargy, loss of pigment in the skin, and thinning, loss, and reddening of the hair. Low levels of protein in the body also cause *edema,* or swelling, which can result in a potbelly appearance. Other abnormalities include liver disease, *anemia,* or low levels of iron, and bulky stools containing undigested food. The lack of available protein also impairs the body's ability to repair itself, to fight disease, and to produce essential proteins such as enzymes and hormones.

This protein deficiency occurs when the child must stop breast-feeding because their mother's milk is required by a newborn infant. The subsequent carbohydrate diet, consisting of foods such as yams and bananas, provides some calories but fails to provide adequate protein. Kwashiorkor often manifests itself in conjunction with inadequate calorie intake or near-starvation, a condition known as *marasmus*.

Kwashiorkor is seen mostly in tropical or subtropical areas such as rural Africa, the Caribbean, and the Pacific Islands. It was first studied as a distinct form of malnutrition in Ghana (then the Gold Coast) by the British physician Cicely Williams, who also introduced the West African term *kwashiorkor* as its medical designation. In Ga, a language of Ghana, this word originally referred to the apparent disease or malign influence from which a child suffered after the birth of a younger sibling.

[From Ga (Niger-Congo language of Ghana) *kwashiɔkɔ.*]

53 logic gate

A device, usually an electrical circuit, that performs one or more logical operations on one or more input signals.

Just as arithmetic operations are performed on numbers, *logical operations* are performed on *truth values.* The two possible truth values are *true* and *false.* One logical operation is *and:* "A and B" is true if A is true and B is true. Similarly, *or* and *not* are logical operations: "A or B" is true if either A or B is true or if both A and B are true; "not A" is true if A is false, and false if A is true. (A and B are the inputs to the logical operations here.) Amazingly enough, the computing power of nearly every computer is built on these three logical operations, which are implemented in the circuitry of logic gates.

Logic gates take small electric signals as inputs. These signals represent the values *true* and *false,* or the binary numbers 1 and 0. The inputs turn electrical switches in the gate on or off, determining the output of the gate. The gates for the logical operations described above are called *and gates, or gates,* and *not gates* (or *inverters*), respectively. Logic gates do the major processing of binary signals in a computer's microprocessor, and together these signals represent not just *true* or *false,* but also numbers, letters, words, images, and sounds.

---

logic gate

SMALL BUT MIGHTY

Typical **logic gates** in a microprocessor are very simple electronic devices, consisting of no more than a few transistors and other components, and their design has grown increasingly subtle as electronic circuitry has been miniaturized. A typical logic gate in a microprocessor is less than one micrometer wide, and a personal computer may contain several million logic gates.

54

magnetosphere (măg-nē′tō-sfîr′)

An asymmetrical region surrounding a planet in which its magnetic field exerts a significant influence. The earth's magnetosphere begins about 100 km (62 mi) above the surface on the side of the earth facing the sun, and it extends hundreds of thousands of kilometers into space on the opposite side.

Because magnetic fields exert a force on electrically charged particles that move through them, most of the charged particles that are emitted by the sun (in the solar wind) and that enter the earth's magnetosphere are deflected away from the earth's surface. But some of these particles are trapped. Some spiral toward the earth's north and south magnetic poles, causing magnetic storms and beautiful auroras, while others follow helical paths back and forth in the Van Allen belts, regions of dangerous radiation high above the earth's surface.

What gives rise to the earth's magnetic field is not well understood. One possibility is the *dynamo theory,* the idea that the motion of the earth's core of liquid iron and nickel, caused by the spinning of the earth and by convection currents, generates the magnetic field.

55

megabyte (měg′ə-bīt′)

1. *A unit of computer memory or data storage capacity equal to 1,048,576 bytes (1,024 kilobytes, or 2^{20} bytes).* **2.** *One million bytes.*

In computer science, the prefix *mega–* often does not have its standard scientific meaning of one million, but refers instead to the power of 2 closest to one million, which is 2^{20}, or 1,048,576. The calculation of data storage capacity (measured in bytes) is based on powers of 2 because of the binary nature of bits (one byte is 8, or 2^3, bits). Thus, a megabyte is properly 1,048,576 bytes, although the term is also used in less specialized contexts to refer to a million bytes. Other terms with numerical prefixes, such as *giga–,* are interpreted similarly. In data transmission, however, transmission rates are measured in bits per second, and calculations are generally based on powers of 10. Thus, a rate of one megabit per second is equal to one million bits per second.

56 melanoma (mĕl′ə-nō′mə)
Plural: **melanomas** or **melanomata**
(mĕl′ə-nō′mə-tə)

A pigmented, usually malignant tumor found most commonly in the skin and arising from a melanin-producing cell.

Malignant melanoma affects one of every 80 Americans, including children and young adults. It is the least common but the most deadly kind of skin cancer because it is not always detected in its early stages and metastasizes quickly to the bone, brain, and liver. The tumor originates from *melanocytes,* cells that produce a dark pigment called *melanin* that is found primarily in the skin, eyes, and hair. Melanoma is most often caused by repeated exposure to the sun and other types of ultraviolet light such as tanning beds. The cancer has been linked to childhood sunburns and is more common in people who have a family history of melanoma or who have light skin, hair, or eyes.

Melanomas are most commonly located on the chest, back, arms, and legs but are also found on the scalp, under the nails, or on the palate. Often they develop from moles. They can be distinguished from noncancerous moles using the *ABCD* criteria: they are *asymmetric* in contour, have irregular *borders*, show variable *color,* and have a *diameter* larger than six millimeters (the size of a pencil eraser). After surgical excision, a melanoma that has metastasized is usually treated with radiation or with immunotherapies such as the drug *interferon.* Metastatic melanoma does not respond well to chemotherapy.

[From New Latin *melanoma . melano ,* black (from Greek *melās, melan-,* black) + New Latin *-ōma* (from Greek *-ōma,* noun suffix).]

mitochondrion (mī′tə-kŏn′drē-ən)
Plural: mitochondria (mī′tə-kŏn′drē-ə)

A structure in the interior of the cells of many organisms in which energy-containing molecules derived from food are broken down in the presence of oxygen to provide energy for the cell.

Some cells can contain up to thousands of mitochondria, which move about in response to the cell's need for chemical energy. The mitochondria provide this energy in the form of *ATP.* Mitochondria have an outer membrane enclosing an inner membrane that has many twists and folds, called *cristae,* that increase the surface area available for carrying out the chemical reactions. Mitochondria have their own DNA that is genetically distinct from the DNA in the cell nucleus. This DNA is similar to bacterial DNA, and it is thought that mitochondria originated as bacterialike organisms that were engulfed by host cells. The ancestors of the mitochondria then entered into a symbiotic relationship with their hosts. The DNA in mitochondria is thus considered a remnant of a past existence as a separate organism.

Sperm and egg cells also contain mitochondria, but in most animals only the mitochondria in the egg survive after fertilization — the mitochondria that helped power the sperm's swim to the egg cell are almost always destroyed. Thus humans inherit their mitochondria only from their mother.

Analysis of mitochondrial DNA (mtDNA) has proved a useful tool in determining the areas in which the modern human species originated and the routes of dispersal that early human groups took around the planet in prehistory. Not only is mitochondrial DNA in some ways easier to study than nuclear DNA, but it also changes very quickly from generation to generation. This results in a relatively large amount of diversity in the mtDNA of a species or a population, which is advantageous when studying the divergence of different subgroups within the population, especially those that have emerged relatively recently.

[New Latin *mitochondrion* : Greek *mitos,* warp thread (probably from Proto-Indo-European **mei-,* to tie) + *khondrion,* diminutive of *khondros,* grain, granule (probably from Proto-Indo-European **grendh-,* to grind, also the source of the English word *grind*).]

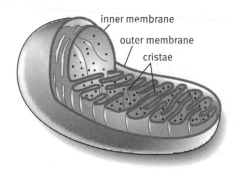

MITOCHONDRION

monotreme (mŏn′ə-trēm′)

A member of the Monotremata, a group of egg-laying mammals whose only living members are the platypus and the three species of echidna.

Monotremes retain some features of the early reptilian organisms from which mammals evolved, features that have been lost in the two other major living groups of mammals, the placental mammals and the marsupials. Monotremes lay eggs, which are leathery and soft-shelled like modern reptile eggs rather than hard-shelled like bird eggs. Like both modern reptiles and birds, monotremes also have a *cloaca*, a single duct that ends in a single exterior orifice and into which the systems used for reproduction, urination, and the excretion of solid waste all open. In the other mammals, the excretory system is separated from the urinary and reproductive systems. Like all mammals, monotremes provide milk for their young, but they have no nipples. Instead, their young lick up the milk that oozes from the mammary (milk-producing) glands in their mother's skin. The average body temperature of monotremes is also lower that that of most other mammal species. The monotremes, however, do not form a "missing link" between the reptilian ancestors of

PLATYPUS
Onithorhynchus anatinus

MODERN MONOTREMES

The only surviving **monotremes** are the three species of echidnas and the single species of platypus. Two species of echidna are found in New Guinea while another inhabits Australia and Tasmania as well as New Guinea. They eat insects and somewhat resemble small porcupines, being covered with spines for defense. Female echidnas incubate their eggs in a pouch. The platypus inhabits environments like riverbanks and lakeshores in Australia and Tasmania. Its ducklike bill has receptors that can detect the small electric fields produced by living organisms and may help it forage in mud to find the worms, crayfish, and other creatures on which it feeds.

mammals on the one hand and their descendants the placental mammals and marsupials, on the other. Instead, they represent another independent branch of the mammalian family tree.

[From Greek *mono-*, one (from Proto-Indo-European **sem-*, one, also the source of Modern English *same* and *some*) + *trēma*, hole, orifice (from Proto-Indo-European **terə-*, turn, rub, also the source of Modern English *drill, thresh,* and *thread*); in reference to the cloaca used for both excretion and reproduction.]

59 monsoon (mŏn-sōōn′)

A system of winds that influences the climate of a large area and that reverses direction with the seasons.

Monsoons are caused primarily by the annual variation in temperature over large areas of land and adjacent ocean water. The variation is much greater over the land than over the water, and the difference results in an excess of atmospheric pressure over the continents in winter, and a deficit in the summer. The disparity causes strong winds to blow between the ocean and the land, bringing heavy seasonal rainfall.

With reference to southern Asia, the word *monsoon* refers to a wind that is part of such a system and that blows from the southwest in the summer, usually bringing heavy rains. In India, the coming of these rains provides welcome relief to the oppressive heat and dust of April and May. Even more importantly, the rains are vital to agriculture in the region. The rice crop is planted at the beginning of the monsoon, and failure of the rains can lead to food shortages.

[From obsolete Dutch *monssoen*, from Portuguese *monção*, from Arabic *mawsim*, time of the year, season, from *wasama*, to mark, *wasuma*, to be(come) beautiful, from the Proto-Semitic root **wsm*, to be(come) fitting, suitable (also the source of the Hebrew month name *Sivan*).]

A FINE MONSOON

The word **monsoon** first appears in English in the late 1500s. It comes from the obsolete Dutch word *monssoen* (now *moesson*), which in turn comes from Portuguese *monção*. Dutch and Portuguese were important languages in the commerce between Asia and Europe that began to flourish in the 1500s after the Portuguese established an overseas route around Africa to India. As the Portuguese mercantile and naval presence in the Indian Ocean increased, they adopted the Arabic word *mawsim*, "season," as a name for the convenient seasonally alternating winds that Arab merchants had long used to bring goods from India to the Arabian Peninsula, eventually to be sold throughout the Near East and Europe. The Arab merchants would set sail to India when the monsoon winds blew in one direction and return to Arabia and Africa when the winds shifted. *Mawsim* has a variety of meanings in Arabic, including "time of the year," "season," "festival," and "harvest." The noun is related to the Arabic verbs *wasama*, "to mark," and *wasuma*, "to be beautiful," and all these words are derived from the Proto-Semitic root **wsm*, "to be fitting." Thus the overarching meaning of *mawsim* could be expressed as "the marked time, the fine time (for doing something)," whether harvesting or holding a festival, or—by later extension—setting sail on a voyage during fair weather.

THE FABRICATING BARON

The term **Munchausen syndrome** comes from *The Surprising Adventures of Baron Munchausen,* a popular storybook about the spectacular travels of its lead character.

The book was originally written as a pamphlet by Rudolph Erich Raspe and published in London in 1785. His fictional hero was based on the real Baron von Münchausen, an 18th century Prussian soldier and sportsman who loved to tell embellished stories about his exploits.

60

Munchausen syndrome (mŭn′chou′zən)

A psychiatric disorder in which a person repeatedly fabricates symptoms and signs of physical illness for the purpose of gaining medical attention.

Munchausen syndrome is a *factitious disorder,* a disorder in which people intentionally make themselves sick or contrive the appearance of illness in order to deceive medical providers and receive care. Munchausen patients usually have a wide knowledge of medicine and either simulate illness (by faking a seizure or putting blood in their urine, for example) or resort to actual self-inflicted injury or infection (such as injecting saliva under the skin to start an infection, intentionally sustaining a burn, or creating skin wounds that look like surgical scars). The ultimate goal is to be admitted to the hospital, often for extensive tests or treatments.

Unlike those who *malinger,* or feign illness to avoid an unwanted circumstance or duty, these individuals have no incentive to be sick other than the compulsive need to be under continuous medical care. Once the symptom or illness is suspected to be factitious, they will often disappear and travel to another doctor or hospital. An even more unfortunate variant of the illness is *Munchausen syndrome by proxy,* in which a parent or other caregiver seeks attention from medical professionals by causing or simulating disease in a child.

The cause of Munchausen syndrome is thought to be an unconscious need to be nurtured as well as to be punished, often stemming from childhood abuse. Because of the deep underlying psychological problems, treatment with psychotherapy is usually unsuccessful. When confronted, pretenders usually move on to a new locale, where they are unrecognized, and doctors start all over again to diagnose their ailments.

[After Baron Karl Friedrich Hieronymus von *Münchausen* (1720–1797), German soldier and raconteur (because the fabricated diseases recall his fictionalized accounts of his life).]

nanotube (năn′ə-tōōb′)

A hollow, cylindrical molecule, usually of carbon.

Nanotubes are one of a class of carbon molecules called *fullerenes,* the discovery of which led to a Nobel Prize in Chemistry in 1996. Fullerenes have a hollow structure made of atoms arranged in alternating pentagons and hexagons. They are extremely small, on the order of a few nanometers (millionths of a millimeter) wide. Like other fullerenes, nanotubes have properties that make them potentially very useful in the creation of extremely small-scale electronic and mechanical devices, one of the goals of an area of research known as *nanotechnology.*

Since they are 50 times stronger than steel, nanotubes are used as reinforcement in certain kinds of concrete and plastics. They have also been spun into fibers that are 20 times stronger than the bullet-resistant material sold as Kevlar. Nanotubes conduct electricity and are considered ideal for building very small, and potentially very fast, computer circuits. Commercial efforts are under way to develop nanotube-based computer memory and displays, among other components. The molecules are already used as additives to plastic in applications that require conductive plastic, as in the brushes of certain kinds of electric motors.

Carbon nanotubes occur naturally in materials such as candle soot, but most applications require molecules with a more regular size and quality, and therefore they are usually synthesized from materials such as graphite. Nonorganic nanotubes have been discovered in clays containing the mineral halloysite, and can be synthesized from boron nitride, which is similar to carbon in many of its properties.

[From *nano-*, extremely small (from Greek *nānos, nannos,* little old man, dwarf) + *tube* (from Latin *tubus*).]

Neanderthal

(nē-ăn′dər-thôl′, nē-ăn′dər-tôl′, *or* nā-än′dər-täl′)
also **Neandertal** (nē-ăn′dər-tôl′
or nā-än′dər-täl′)

*An extinct hominin living throughout most of Europe and in
parts of Asia and northern Africa from around 230,000 to
29,000 years ago.*

Stockily built when compared to anatomically modern humans in order to minimize heat loss, Neanderthals were
adapted to life in the colder environments that prevailed in
these areas during the Pleistocene. Neanderthals have sometimes been considered a species (*Homo neanderthalensis*)
separate from *Homo sapiens* and sometimes a subspecies
(*Homo sapiens neanderthalensis*) of *H. sapiens.* Recent studies
of intact DNA from Neanderthal remains indicate that Neanderthals and anatomically modern humans have been separate lineages on the human family tree for quite a long
time, and that there was probably no interbreeding between
the two groups when they lived in the same areas.

The word *Neanderthal* is sometimes applied metaphori-
cally to a crude, boorish, or slow-witted person, and the
heavy brow ridges typical of their skulls have contributed to
the unscientific image of the "caveman" in popular culture.
The Neanderthal brain, however, was on average slightly
larger overall than that of modern humans, although this
fact may reflect the general tendency of animals living in
colder climates to have slightly larger brains than those living
in warmer areas, as an adaptation to temperature. In recent
years, there has been a great deal of controversy over the
question of whether Neanderthals could speak and use language like modern humans. Nonetheless, Neanderthals
showed considerable cultural sophistication, in that they
controlled fire, made stone tools, and buried their dead with
grave goods.

[After *Neanderthal* (now *Neandertal*), a valley of western Germany
near Düsseldorf, where Neanderthal remains were found in 1856.]

---

nosocomial infection (nō′zə-kō′mē-əl)

An infection that is acquired from a hospital environment.

Patients admitted to a hospital hardly expect to get sick from the facilities and personnel that provide medical care. But every year about 5 percent of hospitalized patients in the United States acquire infections 48 hours or more after hospital admission. Several factors are responsible for hospital-acquired infections. Medical environments have a high prevalence of infectious agents, such as bacteria, viruses, and fungi, that are easily transmitted from one patient to another. Hospital personnel can be the source of these agents when they do not wash their hands properly or when the instruments they use are not properly sterilized. In addition, because illness can weaken the immune system, some patients are particularly susceptible to infections. Many also have skin wounds, catheters, intravenous tubes, or other potential conduits of infection. Others have received *antibiotics,* or infection-fighting drugs, that kill one organism but subsequently allow others to flourish. These organisms are called *opportunists,* and they are the primary cause of nosocomial infections. Opportunistic infections can be especially hard to treat because of antibiotic resistance.

There are 2 million cases of hospital-acquired infections in the United States every year, of which more than 100,000 are fatal. The prevention of this significant public-health problem depends on the implementation of hospital procedures to prevent the transmission of disease-causing organisms. These include protocols for personnel such as wearing gloves and frequent handwashing, maintaining sterility in operating rooms, patient isolation when necessary, and careful handling of body fluids and *fomites,* or contaminated items such as bedding.

[**NOSOCOMIAL:** Ultimately from Greek *nosokomeion*, hospital : *nosos,* illness + *komein,* to tend, take care of. **INFECTION:** Ultimately from Latin *inficere,* to stain, infect.]

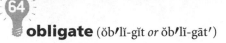

obligate (ŏb′lĭ-gĭt *or* ŏb′lĭ-gāt′)

Capable of existing only in a particular environment, in a particular mode of life, or by engaging in particular behaviors.

An *obligate parasite* is a parasite that cannot survive independently of its host. An *obligate anaerobe* is an organism that cannot survive in the presence of molecular oxygen (O_2), like *Clostridium botulinum,* the bacterium that spoils food in airtight containers and causes botulism. (When exposed to oxygen, this bacterium forms resistant spores and becomes dormant until conditions become more favorable to its growth.) On the other hand, human beings and other animals are *obligate aerobes*—they require oxygen to live.

The term *facultative* is used in contrast to *obligate* and describes organisms capable of existing under varying environmental conditions, in various modes of life, or by assuming various behaviors. Humans are *facultative carnivores.* They can eat meat and very often do so when it is available, but they can remain healthy on a well-balanced vegetarian diet as well.

[Ultimately from Latin *obligāre,* bind, oblige : *ob-,* to, toward, against (from Proto-Indo-European **epi, *opi,* also the source of Greek *epi,* on, at, seen in English words such as *epidermis*) + *ligāre,* to bind (from Proto-Indo-European **leig-,* to bind).]

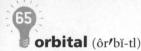

orbital (ôr′bĭ-tl)

A partial description of the quantum state of an electron (or other particle) orbiting the nucleus of an atom.

Early conceptions of the structure of the atom were very different from current models. When it was discovered that light, negatively charged particles (electrons) surrounded a heavy, positively charged core (the nucleus), it was thought that the attractive force between these positive and negative charges would result in circular or elliptical orbits of the electrons around the nucleus, just as moons and other satellites orbit around larger planets. For this reason, the term *orbital* was used to describe the regions in which the electrons move.

But quantum mechanics, a theory that emerged as the structure of the atom was being investigated, changed that picture. According to this theory, an electron in a physical system as small as an atom does not occupy a distinct position, but exists in a cloud of positions, in any one of which it could be detected. Thus, orbitals have no clear boundaries; the shape of an orbital, as depicted graphically, indicates only the regions around the nucleus in which an electron has a relatively high *probability* of being found. Different orbitals have different shapes and orientations, depending on the energy of the electron and other factors (such as its angular momentum).

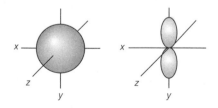

ORBITAL

Two electron orbitals of a hydrogen atom. The nucleus of the atom lies at the intersection of the axes.

pahoehoe (pə-hoi′hoi′)

A type of lava having a smooth, swirled surface. It is highly fluid when molten and spreads out in shiny sheets.

The islands that make up Hawaii were born and bred from volcanoes that rose up over thousands of years from the sea floor. Volcanoes form an important part of the Hawaiian environment, and the Hawaiian language has a variety of words to refer to the effects of volcanism on the landscape. Two of these words have entered English and are used by scientists in naming different kinds of lava flows. One, *pahoehoe,* refers to lava with a ropy or swirled surface. Molten pahoehoe can move very rapidly. When it solidifies, it can form vast smooth plains. The other, *aa,* refers to a type of lava having a rough surface. Aa is relatively slow moving in its molten state, advancing in the form of massive blocks with fissured and angular surfaces that ride on a viscous interior. The blocks range in size between the size of a football and the size of a house. When aa solidifies, it can form very uneven, jagged terrain. Molten pahoehoe can become aa when it begins to cool while still moving and the gasses dissolved in the lava are lost. However, aa does not become pahoehoe.

Pahoehoe comes from the Hawaiian verb *hoe,* "to paddle," since paddles make swirls in the water, while *aa* comes from the Hawaiian word meaning "to burn."

IVAN PAVLOV

Though Ivan Pavlov's (1849–1936) groundbreaking work on conditioning constitutes a major contribution to the field of psychology, he was primarily a medical researcher and made important discoveries in the physiology of the nervous system and digestion. He won the Nobel Prize in Physiology or Medicine in 1904 "in recognition of his work on the physiology of digestion." Psychology, on the other hand, was apparently not something he was interested in; he once wrote that his research in the area of digestion used "ideas borrowed from psychology, but now there is a possibility of its being liberated from such evil influences."

Pavlovian (păv-lō′vē-ən)

Of or relating to classical conditioning, an unconscious learning process by which a person or animal develops a new response to some stimulus because that stimulus is repeatedly paired with something else that naturally elicits the response.

Conditioning is a process in which a person or animal unconsciously learns to respond in some particular way (the *conditioned response*) when it experiences some stimulus (the *conditioned stimulus*). In *classical conditioning,* studied by Ivan Pavlov, learning occurs when some previously neutral conditioned stimulus is repeatedly associated with an *unconditioned stimulus*—a stimulus that elicits a reflexive or instinctive response (the *unconditioned response*). Eventually, the conditioned stimulus alone comes to elicit the reflexive response.

In Pavlov's experiments with dogs, food was an unconditioned stimulus that produced the unconditioned response of salivation. Pavlov repeatedly played a tone to the dogs as a conditioned stimulus when he presented food. The dogs eventually began to salivate when they heard the tone, even when no food was presented. Salivation thus became the conditioned response.

Pavlovian conditioning is a form of learning, in that it represents a change in patterns of behavior based on experience. It nonetheless involves very simple neural mechanisms and occurs even in invertebrate animals. It is distinguished from *operant conditioning,* studied by B. F. Skinner, which involves responses that are reinforced by rewards or punishments.

phenotype (fē′nə-tīp′)

1. *An observable characteristic of an organism, as determined by both genetic makeup and environmental influences.* **2.** *The sum of an organism's observable characteristics.*

The characteristics of an organism are not determined solely by its *genotype*—that is, its genetic makeup. Genes may express themselves differently according to the environment in which the organism lives. For example, the phenotype of the leaves of many buttercup (*Ranunculus*) species varies according to whether they are growing above or below the surface of the water. If they grow underwater, the leaves are finely divided and thread-like, while if they grow above the surface, they are broad. In humans, adult height provides a good example of phenotypic variation, since it is dependent not only on inherited genetic factors but also on nutrition during development. The phenotype of an organism can include not only its physical structure and biochemical makeup, but also its behavior, which is likewise influenced by both genetic and environmental factors.

[From German *Phaenotypus* : Greek *phaino-*, showing (from *phainein,* to show, from Proto-Indo-European **bhā-*, to shine, also the source of English *beacon*) + Greek *tupos,* impression, image, type.]

pheromone (fĕr′ə-mōn′)

A chemical that is secreted by an animal and influences the behavior or development of other animals of that species.

Although an animal's pheromones may consist only of a single chemical compound, they can convey highly specific information to others of the same species, such as prospective mates. For example, when hornets are disturbed, they release an "alarm pheromone" that summons other hornets to their

---

HUMAN PHEROMONES?

Are people affected by **pheromones?** In the 1970s the psychologist Martha McClintock showed that the menstrual cycles of young women living closely together in dormitories tended to occur at the same time every month. This effect was thought by some to be mediated by pheromones. Despite such studies, no pheromone receptors have yet been found in humans.

aid. Some animals, such as cats and dogs, use pheromones to mark territory. These chemicals give information about the animal's species, sex, age, size, and status and indicate how recently it has been present in or visited a certain area. In addition to producing instinctive behavioral responses, pheromones from one individual can actually change another's physiology. For example, queen bees give off a pheromone that inhibits sexual maturation in the other females in the hive. As a result, only the queen can mate and lay eggs.

The pheromone *bombykol,* released by sexually receptive silkworm moths and first isolated in the 1950s, is one of the best-studied examples. It is secreted by the female from a gland in her belly and is detectable by male silkworm moths up to a few miles away. The male identifies the chemical in the environment with tiny receptors at the tip of his antennae and can then locate the female. Female mice also give off pheromones that can arouse males.

[From Greek *pherein,* to carry + English (*hor*)*mone* (from Greek *hormōn,* present participle of *hormān,* to urge on, from *hormē,* impulse).]

photoelectric (fō′tō-ĭ-lĕk′trĭk)

Relating to or exhibiting electrical effects upon exposure to light.

Some photoelectric materials emit electrons upon exposure to certain frequencies of light; others change their electrical properties in other ways. This allows photoelectric devices to convert light signals into electrical signals, as in digital cameras, or to generate electrical power, as in solar cells.

The properties of the photoelectric effect were crucial to the discovery that light takes the form of discrete particles called photons. By the beginning of the 20th century, it had been observed that the light shining on a photoelectric material had to have a certain minimum frequency to induce the effect. The higher the frequency of light, the more energy it has, so it seemed that the electrons needed some minimum amount of energy from the light in order to break free from the material. What was surprising was that increasing the energy by turning up the *intensity* of the light could not induce the effect, even though the light had much more energy. Why not?

In 1906, Albert Einstein proposed a solution to this problem. Assume that light is made up of individual particles, each with a specific energy related only to its frequency. It follows that increasing the intensity of the light of a given frequency means increasing the number of particles being beamed on the material, but not the amount of energy of each particle. Since the particles hit the electrons of the photoelectric material one at a time, like raindrops, then a given particle with enough energy—that is, a high enough frequency—to dislodge an electron will do so as soon as it hits one; if its energy and frequency are too low, it will not. Increasing the number of particles by turning up the intensity of the light therefore has no effect if the frequency of the light is too low, as each individual impact fails to dislodge the electron.

Since light was strongly believed to be a kind of wave, and not a particle, this ingenious solution to the problem baffled physicists at the time. Only with the acceptance of the idea of complementarity and the development of quantum mechanics would this wave-particle duality be understood.

[**PHOTO-**: From Greek *phōto-*, from *phōs, phōt-*, from Proto-Indo-European **bhā-*, to shine (also the source of English *beacon*). **ELECTRIC**: From New Latin *ēlectricus*, deriving from amber, as by rubbing, from Latin *ēlectrum*, amber, from Greek *ēlektron*; in reference to the static electricity generated by rubbing amber.]

MYSTERIES OF LIGHT

💡 Photons cannot be at rest. They always move at the speed of light.

💡 Photons have no mass, but they have measurable momentum, and their paths are distorted by gravitational fields.

💡 Photons have no effect on each other; they pass right through each other without interacting.

💡 Photons have no electric charge themselves, but they interact with charged particles by virtue of their vibrating electrical and magnetic fields.

71

photon (fō′tŏn′)

The subatomic particle that carries the electromagnetic force; the fundamental unit of electromagnetic radiation.

The photon is known as the *quantum* of electromagnetic radiation. In physics, a quantum is a basic, indivisible unit or state that may be present or absent, but never stronger or weaker. Electromagnetic energy, such as light or radio waves, is always emitted and absorbed in such discrete units, that is, as photons. Photons — like all matter — have wavelike properties, the most well-known being that photons can vibrate at different frequencies, distinguishing different colors of light, and visible light from radio waves, microwaves, x-rays, and so on. The higher the frequency, the more energy the photon has. One key to the discovery of photons was the investigation of the photoelectric effect.

Objects with positive or negative electric charge interact with each other by exchanging photons. For this reason photons are called the *carriers* of the electromagnetic force.

piezoelectric effect (pī-ē′zō-ĭ-lĕk′trĭk *or* pē-ā′zō-ĭ-lĕk′trĭk)

The generation of a voltage in certain nonconducting materials, such as quartz crystals and ceramics, when they are subjected to mechanical stress such as pressure or vibration.

The molecules of many crystals are polarized, meaning that one side of the molecule has a more negative charge, and the other side a more positive charge. Applying stress to the crystal reorients the molecules and displaces their electric charges, resulting in measurable voltage.

All piezoelectric materials also exhibit the *reverse piezoelectric effect.* Placing them in an electric field causes their molecules to tend to align themselves with it, and depending on the orientation and arrangement of the molecules, this can cause the material to expand, contract, or twist.

Piezoelectric materials have many uses in the technology that surrounds us. Quartz, for example, vibrates at a precise frequency with very little variation when exposed to a fluctuating electric field, making it useful in time-keeping devices in electronic clocks and computers. High-frequency vibrations from piezoelectric devices have been used in sonar systems to generate the chirps whose echos reveal the presence and position of other objects in the water. Sonograms used in medical imaging, especially during pregnancy, are generated by measuring the intensity with which high frequency vibrations pass through the body; these vibrations are detected and generated through the piezoelectric and reverse piezoelectric effects. Rochelle salt, which generates a fairly high voltage even under low stress, was used in early microphones to convert mechanical vibrations into electrical signals, and similar materials such as lead titanate are used in modern transducers for musical instruments.

[From *piezo-*, pressure (from Greek *piezein*, to press tight, squeeze, from Proto-Indo-European **pi-sed-yo-*, to sit upon, from **sed-*, to sit, also the source of Modern English *sit*) + *electric.*]

placebo (plə-sē′bō)

Plural: **placebos** or **placeboes**

A substance containing no medication and prescribed to reinforce a patient's expectation of getting well or used as a control in a clinical research trial to determine the effectiveness of a potential new drug.

The mind has significant potential to contribute to the healing of the body. One of the most clear demonstrations of this potential is in the *placebo effect*—the improvement of a patient that follows treatment but arises from the patient's expectations concerning the treatment rather than from the treatment itself. Groups of patients who are given substances that are known to have no direct physiological effect in the treatment of disease, such as sugar pills, often show greater rates of improvement than those of patients given no treatment at all. This difference in improvement is usually attributed to the patients' belief that the treatment will be effective.

The existence of the placebo effect is one reason that placebos are sometimes used in *clinical trials*—research studies designed to test the effectiveness of potential new medicines. In order to prove that a drug is effective against a disease, such studies compare the rate of improvement in an *experimental group*—a group of patients given the drug—to the rate of improvement in a *control group*—a group of patients that is similar in relevant respects to the experimental group but is given a placebo instead of the drug. In this way, if the experimental group does show a higher rate of improvement, researchers know that it is not simply the result of the placebo effect.

[Latin *placēbō*, I shall please (the patient by prescribing medicine).]

prion (prī′ŏn *or* prē′ŏn)

A microscopic protein particle that is capable of self-replication and causes degenerative diseases of the nervous system.

In 1997 Stanley Prusiner was awarded a Nobel Prize for theorizing that a misshapen form of a harmless protein thought to be involved in synaptic function could be an agent of infection. These deviant proteins are called *prions,* and although they contain no genetic material, they replicate themselves like the nucleic acids contained in DNA and RNA. The discovery of prion replication, which results in the reproduction of strings of amino acids, is an exception to one of the central tenets of biology—that chemical self-replication is limited to nucleic acids. The exact mechanism of prion replication is not clearly understood.

Prions cause healthy proteins to misfold and aggregate in the brain, resulting in diseases called *spongiform encephalopathies* because they leave the brain riddled with holes. In animals, prions cause *scrapie* in sheep and bovine spongiform encephalopathy, known as *mad cow disease,* in cattle. In humans, *kuru,* associated with cannibalism, and *Creutzfeldt-Jakob disease* are among several neurodegenerative diseases thought to be caused by prions. All of these diseases are characterized by a loss of motor control, paralysis, dementia, and eventual death because of massive destruction of brain tissue.

The term *prion* was coined by Stanley Prusiner himself by taking elements from the phrase *pro(teinaceous) in(fectious particle).* Simple abbreviation of this phrase, using the first few letters of each word, would result in *proin,* but Prusiner altered this to *prion,* which he believed sounded better.

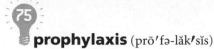

prophylaxis (prō′fə-lăk′sĭs)
    Plural: **prophylaxes** (prō′fə-lăk′sēz′)

Any of various measures intended to prevent illness or injury.

Prophylaxis encompasses a wide range of medical, surgical, and dental procedures that prevent a person or animal from getting sick or hurt. Sometimes people get prophylactic treatment when they are completely well, such as vaccinations for tetanus, hepatitis vaccines for foreign travel, or dental cleanings. Antibiotics are often given before surgery to prevent infections. Other times prophylaxis is reserved for people who are at high risk for a certain condition, such as elderly or asthmatic patients who get flu vaccines. People who have been exposed to an infection can receive prophylactic drugs to avoid contracting it. Prophylaxis can be very simple. Walking inside a plane during a long flight, for example, helps to prevent blood clots. Wearing a helmet while riding a bicycle or motorcycle prevents injury from accidents.

[Ultimately from Greek *prophylassein,* to take precautions against : *pro-,* before + *phulassein,* to protect.]

🔆 protein folding

The process by which proteins assume various three-dimensional shapes in the body, allowing them to perform vital and specialized biochemical functions.

Proteins are complex organic chemical compounds, such as enzymes, hormones, and antibodies, that form the basis of living tissues and are essential to life. The building blocks of proteins are 20 *amino acids,* simpler groups of molecules that join together into chains and that are connected by chemical links called *peptide bonds.* These chemical chains, however, are hardly linear. As a result of forces of attraction and repulsion between atoms in the chains, amino acids form molecular bonds with nonadjacent molecules, resulting in twisting and kinking. Thus, proteins are folded into complex and distinct shapes.

One common structure is the *alpha helix,* a single, spiral chain of amino acids that forms a coil. Another protein structure is the *beta sheet,* characterized by two or more parallel adjacent polypeptide chains arranged in a zigzag pattern that results in one straight chain. In both of these structures, the shapes are stabilized by hydrogen bonds that form between molecules in the chains. *Random coils* are sequences of amino acids that are neither helixes nor beta-sheets. When the alpha-helical or beta-sheet proteins *denature,* or structurally unfold because of exposure to heat or other chemicals, they become random coils.

Protein folding is extremely important because a protein's shape defines its function in essential biochemical processes. The shape of hemoglobin, for example, is ideal for transporting oxygen molecules in the bloodstream. Similarly, some proteins fold to fit exactly into cell receptors where they participate in essential aspects of cell metabolism. Misfolded proteins have been implicated in certain medical conditions such as Alzheimer's disease, Parkinson's disease, and mad cow disease.

protolanguage (prō′tō-lăng′gwĭj)

A language that is the ancestor of another language or a group of languages, especially when this ancestral language is not recorded in writing.

The sounds, vocabulary, and grammar of all living languages change over time, in much the same way that animal or plant species evolve. One language can even develop into several distinct languages. When linguists suspect that a group of languages may descend from a common ancestor and form a *language family,* they attempt to *reconstruct* this ancestor, the protolanguage, by comparing the various features of the known languages that may have descended from it. Based on correspondences between the known languages, they propose *protoforms*—hypothetical words or word building-elements such as roots—from which the words of the later languages can be derived by well-established principles of language change.

Proto-Indo-European, the ancestor of English as well as many other languages of modern and ancient Europe and India, is one of the most well-known and successful examples of a reconstructed protolanguage. Scholars at the end of the 18th century noticed striking similarities among groups of words in many languages of Europe and India. For example, the English word *knee* (from Old English *cnēo*) resembles Latin *genū,* Greek *gonu,* Sanskrit *jānu,* all meaning "knee." English *foot* (from Old English *fōt*) resembles Latin *pedem,* Greek *poda,* and Sanskrit *pādam,* all meaning "foot." (These last three words for foot are given in the form they would have as direct objects in a sentence.) Scholars also noted that the differences between the words were not random: one particular sound in one language usually corresponds to another particular sound in another language. Wherever most of the Indo-European languages have a hard *g,* English has a *k*-sound. For example, the *k*-sound in English *cold* matches the *g* in Latin *gelāre,* "to freeze," the ultimate source of English words like *congeal* and *gelato.* (English used to have a *k*-sound in *knee,* as the spelling still indicates.) Wherever the other languages often have a *p,* as in Latin *pater,* Greek *patēr,* and Sanskrit *pitā,* all meaning "father," English has an *f,* as in *father.* There are many other such regular sound correspondences among the Indo-European languages. Based on these facts, linguists reconstruct Proto-Indo-European roots like **gel-,* "to freeze," and nouns like **genu-,* "knee," **ped-,* "foot," and **pətēr-,* "father." The Eng-lish words derive from these protoforms by regular sound changes, such as those that turned *g*-sounds to *k*-sounds and *p*-sounds to *f*-sounds.

Linguists have reconstructed the protolanguages of many other language families all over the world, such as the Semitic family (including Arabic and Hebrew), the Uto-Aztecan family (including Hopi and Nahuatl, the language of the Aztecs), and the Austronesian family (including Malay and Hawaiian). Almost all the one hundred words discussed in this book can be traced, either wholly or in part, to a Proto-Indo-European or a Proto-Semitic root, and where practicable, these roots have been included in the etymologies at the end of each entry.

[**PROTO:** From Greek *prōtos,* first, from Proto-Indo-European **per-,* the base of words with meanings like "forward," (also the source of English *first*). **LANGUAGE:** From Old French *langage,* from *langue,* tongue, language, from Latin *lingua,* from Proto-Indo-European *dṇghū-,* tongue (also the source of English *tongue*).]

quantum mechanics

A fundamental theory of matter and energy, especially at atomic and subatomic scales, in which many physical phenomena are understood to take on discrete values or take the form of discrete particles called quanta.

One of the most surprising things about the fundamental nature of the physical world is that all matter displays both wavelike and particlelike properties. Light, for instance, famously acts like a vibrating wave (an electromagnetic wave of electric and magnetic fields vibrating at some frequency). Yet light also carries momentum, and bounces off things as if it were a tiny particle. Moreover, the intensity of light at a given frequency cannot be continuously reduced: it always jumps up and down by discrete energy levels. Quantum mechanics resolves this apparent contradiction with the concept of the *photon,* a quantum of electromagnetic energy.

Another surprising thing about the physical world is that it behaves probabilistically. In quantum mechanics, particles in a physical system (such as an electron in an *orbital* of an atom) are described with a *wave function* (which captures the wavelike nature of the particle). The wave function sketches out the regions in space where the particle might be observed to have an effect (which captures the more particlelike nature of the particle), and what the probability of that observation would be.

Some scientists maintain that verbal descriptions of quantum mechanics can never do justice to its basic concepts and that only familiarity with the mathematical formalism of the theory can provide a genuine understanding of it.

79 **radiometric dating** (rā′dē-ō-mĕt′rĭk)

A method for determining the age of an object based on the concentration of a particular radioactive isotope contained within it.

The most well-known kind of radiometric dating is *carbon* or *radiocarbon dating,* by which the age of organic materials, such as the remains or fossils of plants and animals, can be determined. The technique is quite straightforward. It is known that a certain, very small amount of the carbon in air is an isotope called carbon 14. Carbon 14 behaves chemically just like regular carbon (carbon-12), but it is slightly heavier, having a total of 14 protons and neutrons in its nucleus rather than the normal 12. Its heaviness makes it unstable, and it undergoes radioactive decay. Since living things exchange carbon with the air around them and with other living things (by eating them), they have the same percentage of carbon 14 in them as the air. But when a living thing dies (and is not consumed by other living things), it stops exchanging carbon with its surroundings. Since radioactive carbon decays over time at a known rate (its half-life is 5,780 years), measuring how much of it is left in the remains of a living thing gives an estimate of the amount of time since its death.

For inorganic materials containing radioactive materials, such as rocks containing radioactive rubidium, the amount of the radioactive material in the object is compared to the amount of the decay products (in this case strontium). The object's approximate age can then be figured out using the known rate of decay of the isotope: the more decay product, the older the material.

---

80 rain shadow

An area having relatively little precipitation due to the effect of a topographic barrier, especially a mountain range, that causes the prevailing winds to lose their moisture on the windward side. This in turn causes the leeward side to be dry.

When a moving mass of warm, moist air encounters a range of mountains, it rises to pass over them. As it rises, it encounters lower atmospheric pressure, which in turn causes the air to expand and cool. As the air cools, it loses its ability to hold water vapor. The air eventually becomes saturated with water vapor that then condenses out in the form of precipitation falling on the windward side of the mountain. When the air, now dry, descends the leeward slopes of the mountains, it is compressed and warmed. Since warm air can hold more water vapor, the air is now far from being saturated and precipitation rarely occurs. This process is what makes Death Valley, the driest place in North America. Death Valley lies in the rain shadow of the Sierra Nevada mountains.

[**RAIN:** From Old English *regn, rēn,* from Proto-Indo-European **reg-, *rek-,* moist (possibly also the source of Latin *rigāre,* to water, source of English *irrigate*). **SHADOW:** From Old English *sceaduwe,* genitive, dative, and accusative singular of *sceadu,* shade, shadow, from Proto-Indo-European **skot-,* dark, shade.]

refraction (rĭ-frăk′shən)

The change in the direction of motion of a wave, such as a light, water, or sound wave, as it passes from a region where it travels at one speed to a region where it travels at a different speed.

Light, for example, is an electromagnetic wave made of vibrating electrical and magnetic fields. When it passes through matter, it interacts with the charged particles that atoms are made of (the protons and electrons). This interaction tends to slow the light down; different materials slow light down to different degrees.

We tend to perceive the position of the things we see as if the light reflected off them had traveled in a straight line to our eyes. Because of this, a bend in the path of the light can make an object appear to be displaced or distorted. For example, refraction of light passing from dense water to lighter air makes a pencil in a glass of water appear to be bent or broken, and the body of a swimmer underwater looks flattened out from above the surface due to refraction.

REFRACTION

Light waves bend as they pass from one substance to another. This pencil appears to be bent or broken due to the different paths taken by light from the pencil, through the air only, through air and glass, and through water, air, and glass.

BREAKING WAVES
AND SHIMMERING SANDS

Why do ocean waves break parallel to the shore, no matter which direction they originally come from? **Refraction** changes their direction. As the waves move ashore, they are gradually slowed by the increasingly shallow water, so any wave coming in at an angle is refracted directly into the shoreline.

Refraction of blue light from the sky, passing from dense, cool upper air into light, hot air near the surface of hot sand or asphalt, can be strong enough to bend the light back up again, so that the surface itself appears to shimmer with blue, like the surface of water reflecting the blue sky.

REM sleep (rĕm)

Short for rapid eye movement sleep. *A period of sleep characterized by rapid periodic twitching movements of the eye muscles and other physiological changes, such as accelerated respiration and heart rate, increased brain activity, and muscle relaxation.*

REM sleep is the fifth and last stage of sleep that occurs in the *sleep cycle,* which repeats itself about five times throughout a period of sleep. Brain activity decreases over the first four stages, known collectively as *non-REM sleep,* but is heightened during REM sleep. REM sleep is the stage in which most dreaming takes place and is thought to allow for the organization of memories and the retention of learning. REM stages become longer with each sleep cycle and account for about 20 to 25 percent of total sleep in adult humans. In infants, roughly 50 percent of sleep is REM sleep, which is believed to be necessary for the maturation of the central nervous system.

REM sleep has been detected in placental mammals, marsupials, and birds, and characteristics of it have been shown in monotremes. The amount of REM sleep that an animal requires varies widely even between closely related species and surprisingly does not appear to be connected with intelligence. For example, REM sleep in primates can range from 0.7 to 1.9 hours per day out of a total sleep time of 8 to 17 hours, whereas rodents, whose total sleep ranges from 7 to 16 hours per day, spend 0.8 to 3.4 hours in REM sleep. It is thought that the maturity of a species' young at birth is the major factor in determining REM sleep patterns. This accounts for the fact that marsupials such as kangaroos, whose young are born immature and develop externally in a pouch, require some of the greatest amounts of REM sleep.

retrovirus (rĕt′rō-vī′rəs)
Plural: retroviruses

A virus that stores its genetic information as RNA molecules, rather than DNA, and that uses its RNA to form DNA when it infects a cell.

Retroviruses and other *RNA viruses* are unique in that they have RNA as their genetic material. In most organisms, genetic information is stored as DNA, and DNA is used to form RNA. This process, called *transcription,* is the first step in creating the proteins that regulate the normal growth and development of a cell. When a virus infects a cell, it interferes with the process, using the cell to reproduce its own genetic material.

Retroviruses got their name because they reverse the normal flow of information from DNA to RNA. When they infect a cell, a process called *reverse transcription* occurs: An enzyme carried by the virus creates DNA from the virus's RNA. This viral DNA then gets copied into the infected cell's DNA, and uses the cell's own processes to copy itself.

Like all RNA viruses, retroviruses mutate quickly. RNA is less stable than DNA, which means that errors in duplicating it occur more frequently. These frequent changes in genetic makeup mean that RNA viruses evolve faster than any other organism, and are thus often able to elude the immune systems of the organisms they infect. HIV (*human immunodeficiency virus*), the virus that causes AIDS, is a retrovirus. Its very fast mutation rate (new strains occur in a matter of weeks) makes it very difficult to develop a vaccine for HIV.

[Ultimately from Latin *retrō-*, backward (in reference to the reverse transcription of DNA from RNA) + *vīrus,* slime, poison, virus.]

roentgenium

(rĕnt′gən′ē-əm *or* rŭnt′jən′ē-əm)

Symbol: **Rg.** *A heavy, synthetic chemical element with an atomic number of 111.*

Roentgenium, formerly called *ununium* (after the Latin for "one one one," referring to the number of protons in the atom's nucleus), is the heaviest known chemical element. As is the case with all super-heavy elements (elements that have more protons and neutrons than uranium), roentgenium atoms are unstable and highly radioactive: the attractive force between protons and neutrons isn't strong enough to hold so many of them together. For this reason, the most stable roentgenium atoms have a half-life of only 3.6 seconds; a trillion roentgenium atoms would decay in less than 30 seconds. Not surprisingly, such an unstable element has never been found on earth and has been created only in the laboratory. Some scientists speculate that if enough roentgenium could be produced to be seen, it would be gold in color, but we will probably never know for sure.

[After Wilhelm Conrad *Roentgen* (1845-1923), German physicist and discoverer of x-rays.]

sex

Either of two categories, male and female, that characterize the reproductive structures and functions of many organisms. Males produce small, mobile reproductive cells (sperm), while females produce larger, less mobile reproductive cells (eggs).

Thanks to high school biology, most of us are familiar with the X and Y sex chromosomes found in humans and other mammals, in which males are XY and females XX. Birds as well have two sex chromosomes, called W and Z. Male birds are ZZ while females are ZW. Such chromosomal sex determination, however, is far from being a universal principal. In bees and wasps, females develop from fertilized eggs while males develop from unfertilized eggs. Among many other organisms, sex is determined by environmental factors. The developing offspring in the eggs of the American alligator become males when incubated at above 34°C (93°F), but females when incubated below 30°C (86°F), while the midrange of temperatures results in both males and females.

Another example of environmental sex determination is provided by a species of slipper limpet, a kind of mollusk in which all individuals begin life as females. Clinging to rocks and to each other, they form tall piles, and the limpet on top of the pile changes into a male. The eggs of these slipper limpets are fertilized within the female, and the male on top extends his reproductive organ down the pile of females to fertilize them. If another limpet attaches itself atop the male limpet, the newcomer becomes male, and the male limpet beneath it reverts to being female. The same individual can thus make eggs and sperm at different times in its life. Such animals are not *hermaphrodites* (organisms that produce both sperm and eggs at once)—instead, they change sex.

A few species have only one sex. Some species of lizards reproduce only by *parthenogenesis*—their unfertilized eggs grow into adults, and these species no longer have males. The offspring are in fact clones of their mother.

sociobiology (sō'sē-ō-bī-ŏl'ə-jē)

The scientific study of the biological basis of the social behavior of animals, based on the theory that such behavior is influenced by genes and that the genes influencing behavior are subject to the usual mechanisms of evolution.

Sociobiologists seek to find explanations for such animal behaviors as aggression and altruism in relation to the survival of the animal's genes in the gene pool. For example, an individual squirrel may have a gene that contributes to an altruistic behavior like giving a warning call to others about the approach of a predator. The warning cry may alert the predator of the exact position of the squirrel that gives warning and make it more likely that the predator will catch the squirrel. According to a preliminary, superficial analysis, such altruistic behavior may appear detrimental to the survival of the squirrel's genes in the next generation. However, other squirrels closely related to the first squirrel may escape the predator on account of the first squirrel's warning. Altruistic behavior, although detrimental to the squirrel giving warning, thus helps increase the reproductive success of a closely related individuals, some of which also carry the gene influencing altruistic behavior. This gene will then tend to spread in the gene pool. In this way, sociobiology has provided explanations for many aspects of animal societies that would otherwise be puzzling, such as the existence in ant colonies of female workers who do not reproduce but instead devote themselves to the task of maintaining the colony and nurturing their siblings.

There has been considerable controversy about how far the methods of sociobiology can be applied to human behavior. Many scientists have pointed out the dangerous social consequences posed by a superficial understanding of sociobiology or the simplistic, nonscientific concept of "genes for behaviors," as opposed to the scientific concept of "genes that influence behavior."

[**SOCIO-:** From French, from Latin *socius,* companion, from Proto-Indo-European **sek^w-*, to follow. **BIOLOGY:** Ultimately from Greek *bios,* life (from Proto-Indo-European **gʷeiə-*, to live, also the source of English *quick*) + Greek *-logiā,* -logy (from *logos,* word, speech, and from *-logos,* one who deals with, both from *legein,* to pick up, recount, speak, from Proto-Indo-European **leg-*, to gather).]

87 solar wind

A continuous stream of plasma ejected by a star, especially the sun, flowing outward from the corona. The solar winds of stars in general are sometimes called stellar winds.

This plasma, which consists mostly of protons and electrons, has enough energy to escape the sun's gravitational field at speeds averaging 1,610,000 km (1,000,000 mi) per hour. The speed and intensity of the solar wind depend on magnetic activity and motion on the surface of the sun; solar flares, for example, can produce especially strong solar winds, enough sometimes to disrupt electronic communication on the earth. The tails of comets, which always extend away from the sun regardless of the direction of the comet's motion, are a result of the impact of solar wind, which dislodges ice and other particles from the comet's surface.

Solar winds can sometimes be seen. Strong solar winds, especially after solar flares, that pass near the earth are deflected by the earth's magnetic fields, especially near the poles, where the charged particles of the solar wind tend to circulate and converge. When they collide with the earth's upper atmosphere, solar winds give rise to the amazing sight of the *auroras,* such as the northern lights.

superposition

The principle by which the description of the state of a physical system can be broken down into descriptions that are themselves possible states of the system.

Superposition is usually fairly straightforward. For example, the vibration of a plucked guitar string is made of one main note, together with numerous overtones called *harmonics*. The various tones exist in superposition with each other. The complex vibration of the string can be thought of as the sum of these simple vibrations, each of which can occur independently of the others (in fact, with certain finger techniques, it is possible to play the harmonics individually).

In quantum mechanics, superposition has some strange consequences. For example, a photon—a single particle of light—that passes through a screen with two slits in it can be described as if it were following two possible paths, one for each slit. The photon is considered to be in a superposition of these two states, each state following one path. But these paths, having passed through the slits, may cross each other again, and the wavelike properties of the photon then create interference effects between the two paths (such as an interference pattern on another screen that the photon strikes). Thus, because of superposition, a single photon can literally interfere with itself!

telomere (tĕl′ə-mîr′)

Either of the sections of DNA occurring at the ends of a chromosome.

The DNA in the telomeres in our chromosomes is not coding DNA — that is, it does not contain instructions for manufacturing the proteins that make up our bodies and help carry out the physical processes within them. When the DNA of one of our chromosomes is replicated as part of the creation of new cells, the enzymes that make new copies of the DNA stop copying before the end of the chromosome. Telomeres ensure that the enzymes will go all the way to the end of the useful (coding) DNA before stopping replication. In the cell of an embryo, the telomeres are continually renewed with each cell division, until the embryonic cell becomes specialized as a particular kind of cell within the body. Then, however, the telomeres of the specialized cell begin to shorten with each cellular division. Eventually the telomeres become too short and leave the chromosomes with "loose ends." The cell then enters *senescence* — it can no longer divide as part of bodily growth and maintenance. Moreover, the "loose ends" of the chromosomes may be mistakenly connected together as part of ongoing repair processes within the cell, and this leads to genetic damage. As more and more cells enter senescence and genetic damage accumulates, the body begins to deteriorate. Thus the shortening of telomeres plays a role in aging and in the development of cancers.

[From Greek *telos,* end, completion of a cycle (from Proto-Indo-European *k^wel-, to turn, also the source of English *wheel*) + *meros,* part, share (from Proto-Indo-European *(s)mer-,* to get a share, also the source of English *merit,* from Latin *merēre, merērī,* deserve, obtain).]

teratogen (tə-răt′ə-jən)

An agent that causes structural or functional damage to a fetus or an embryo.

Teratogens are prenatal *toxins,* or poisons, that can cause congenital malformations, intrauterine growth retardation, cancer, or death in a developing *embryo* (unborn offspring up to eight weeks after conception) or *fetus* (unborn offspring from eight weeks until birth). The process of *teratogenesis* occurs most frequently between the third and eighth week after conception, when body organs are being formed. Teratogens include drugs, chemicals, viruses, and radiation. They can affect the embryo or placenta directly or cause maternal illness that adversely affects the embryo.

Alcohol, the most common teratogen, causes a variety of defects including *fetal alcohol syndrome,* a condition characterized by mental retardation, growth retardation, cranial and facial malformations, and heart defects. The *rubella* virus, which causes German measles, usually causes mild symptoms in pregnant women and other adults but is a potent teratogen that can cause multiple fetal defects and fetal death.

Many over-the-counter and prescription drugs have teratogenic effects and should be avoided during pregnancy. *DES (diethylstilbestrol),* a hormonal drug given to women in early pregnancy to prevent miscarriages in the 1940s and 1950s, was found to cause vaginal cancer and other gynecologic abnormalities in adolescent girls whose mothers received the drug. *Thalidomide,* a drug prescribed in the 1960s for symptoms of nausea during early pregnancy, was later found to cause stunting or absence of the limbs. Today, prescription drugs are specifically categorized for safety during pregnancy.

[From *terato-,* malignancy (from Greek, from *teras, terat-,* portent, monster) + *-gen,* producer (from Greek *-genēs,* born, from Proto-Indo-European **genə-,* to give birth, also the source of Modern English *kin, kindred,* and *kind*).]

theory

A set of statements or principles devised to explain a group of facts or phenomena.

Most theories that are accepted by scientists have been repeatedly tested by experiments and can be used to make predictions about natural phenomena. A theory is not something that can be proven true, but it can be verified beyond reasonable doubt in the context of one's fundamental beliefs. Scientists must always be prepared to abandon a theory for a better one. Newton's theories of motion, for example, were very precise, accurate, and mathematically rigorous, describing what Newton thought were the laws of motion. Yet these laws have been superseded by Einstein's ideas, formulated in his Theory of Relativity.

Interestingly, scientific *facts* are part of the description of the world used in a theory, so facts, like theories, change over time. The "obvious fact" that the sun revolves around the earth was shown to be highly theoretical, indeed part of a theory that virtually no one accepts any more.

[Ultimately from Greek *theōriā*, from *theōros*, spectator : probably *theā*, a viewing + *-(h)oros*, seeing (from *horān*, to see).]

tidal force

A secondary effect of the gravitational forces between two objects, such as the earth and moon, that tends to elongate each body along the axis of a line connecting their centers.

Tidal forces are the result of variation in the strength and the direction of the force of gravity across the affected object. The first and most important component of tidal force stems from the weakening of gravity as one moves away from the attracting source. This results in greater gravitational pull on the near side of the object than on the far side, yielding a net *tidal force* that stretches the object. A second net tidal force arises because the force of gravity on an object at every point is oriented toward a single point at the center of the attracting body. This means that there is a net force squeezing the body together in the middle (perpendicular to the elongation of the first tidal force). These pulling and squeezing effects of tidal forces on the earth caused by the moon (and to a lesser degree the sun) are the major forces that drive the earth's tides, which rise and fall as the earth rotates.

The earth in turn induces tidal forces on the moon. But because of the earth's larger size, these tidal forces, in addition to affecting the shape of the moon, have gradually slowed the moon's rotation until it has become synchronized with its period of revolution around the earth—so that now the same side of the moon always faces the earth. Because of tidal forces, most moons in the solar system exhibit synchronous rotation.

time dilation

The slowing of a clock with respect to an observer.

Einstein's Theory of Relativity can be thought of as a theory of the "shape" of space and time, and it makes predictions about how this shape appears to different observers in different situations. According to this theory, there are cases in which one person's clock, which appears to that person to be ticking at a constant rate, appears to another observer to be ticking more slowly than his own clock—even though the clocks are calibrated to tick at the same rate. The first situation is when one person's clock has accelerated into motion with respect to the observer. The other is when the person and his clock undergo an accelerative force, as when accelerating through space or when under the influence of gravity, that the observer does not undergo. Conversely, the person who has undergone an acceleration or undergoes an accelerative force observes other clocks to be ticking more quickly than his own. Experiments have verified that the clock in a balloon high above the earth, where the force of gravity is weaker, runs faster, from our point of view on earth, than our own clocks. Also, the clocks of fast-moving spacecraft run noticeably slower than our own clocks. These differences are very small but detectable.

Universal Time

The time at the prime meridian, measured by the apparent movement of the celestial sphere; the basis of a worldwide system of standard times primarily used by astronomers.

The worldwide system of standard times is based on the time at the *prime meridian* (the zero line of longitude), which goes through Greenwich, England. Times for all time zones on the globe are determined by adding to, or subtracting from, the time at Greenwich. While the name of this time was officially changed to Universal Time (UT) in 1928, the term Greenwich Mean Time (GMT) is still common.

Before the introduction of atomic clocks, all time measurement was based on measuring the rotation of the earth, with one day being equal to one complete rotation. Rotations are counted by tracking the apparent motion of either the sun or, as in the case of UT, the *celestial sphere* (the imaginary sphere on which the stars, planets, and other heavenly bodies appear to be located). In fact, Greenwich first became the prime meridian because it was the site of the Royal Greenwich Observatory, renowned for its ability to make the precise astronomical measurements necessary to keep accurate time.

Because the earth's rotation changes speed slightly over the course of a year, the decision was made in 1960 to begin keeping time with atomic clocks, which measure time by using the very uniform frequency of radiation emitted or absorbed by a given element when it changes quantum state. The current basis of standard times—Coordinated Universal Time (UTC)—is the time at Greenwich as measured by atomic clocks. Because the earth's rotation is also gradually slowing due to tidal friction, leap seconds are added occasionally to keep UTC coordinated with the earth's rotation.

95
urea (yŏŏ-rē′ə)

A chemical compound (N_2H_4CO) that is the chief nitrogen-containing waste product excreted in the urine of mammals and some fish.

Urea is the final nitrogenous (nitrogen-containing) product formed by the breakdown of proteins in the human body, during which amino groups (NH_2) are removed from amino acids and converted into ammonium ions (NH_4). Ammonium ions are very toxic at high concentrations, and the liver converts them into urea, which is less toxic. The urea produced by the liver then circulates in the blood until it is filtered out by the kidneys and excreted in the urine.

Many aquatic organisms, especially those that live in fresh water, excrete ammonium ions from their bodies directly into their environment soon after they are formed, but this requires the availability of a great deal of water. Terrestrial animals, however, are faced with the problem of limited availability of water for excretion. Mammals convert ammonium ions into the less toxic urea so that nitrogenous waste can build up in the body before it is concentrated in urine and excreted. Reptiles and birds, on the other hand, convert ammonium ions to *uric acid,* which is even less toxic than urea. Uric acid also requires much less water than urea to be excreted, and the white pasty portion of a bird dropping is in fact the bird's urine, consisting mostly of uric acid. The conversion of nitrogenous waste to uric acid, which requires more energy on the organism's part than conversion to urea, is probably an adaptation to laying eggs on dry land. Within the egg, the developing reptile or bird has a limited water supply, and it must also store its waste within the egg until it hatches. The conversion of waste to uric acid allows the developing animal to conserve water within the egg and keeps it from being poisoned by the accumulation of waste.

[New Latin, from French *urée*, from *urine,* urine, from Old French, from Latin *ūrīna,* from Proto-Indo-European *wēr-*, water, liquid.]

---

stigial (vĕ-stĭj′ē-əl *or* vĕ-stĭj′əl)

…elating to a body part or behavior that has become degenerate
…r rudimentary and has lost its primary use because of evolu-
tionary change.

Whales have small bones located in the muscles of their body walls that are vestigial bones of hips and hind limbs. The ancestors of whales, animals related to hippos, originally lived on land and had four limbs, but they lost their external hind legs as part of the evolution of a streamlined shape adapted to swimming.

The human appendix appears to be a vestige of an organ that helped our distant mammalian ancestors to digest cellulose, the compound of which plant cell walls are made. The appendix arises from the cecum, the saclike beginning of the large intestine. In humans, this organ absorbs water and minerals from digested food, but in many other mammals the cecum, often with a long associated appendix, houses cellulose-digesting bacteria. In mammal species that eat mostly plant leaves and stems, such as rabbits or horses, the cecum and its associated appendix (if present) are usually much larger and more developed than in humans. Although the distant primate ancestors of humans may have had cellulose-rich diets and correspondingly larger ceca, humans eat a greater variety of foods, and the human cecum and appendix no longer house cellulose-digesting bacteria. The appendix contains lymphoid tissue that is similar to that found elsewhere in the intestinal tract and may play a role in immune function, but the removal of the human appendix has no apparent adverse effects. In many species of carnivores, such as dogs, the cecum and appendix have become even more reduced and are sometimes completely absent.

[Ultimately from Latin *vestīgium,* footprint, trace, vestige + *-ālis,* adjectival suffix.]

wave function

A mathematical function used in quantum mechanics to describe the propagation of the wave that is associated with a particle or group of particles.

The idea that all matter behaves both as if it were made out of particles and as if it were made out of waves strikes us as peculiar, even 100 years after scientists began to face these apparently contradictory properties head on. Waves are extended, continuous things, while particles are hard, indivisible, knobby things. Classical physics offered no way to reconcile them into one picture, but the experimental facts demanded a solution.

The wave function is a part of the answer. In quantum mechanics, a particle in a physical system may be modeled by a function, the wave function, so called because it describes wavelike patterns extending and fluctuating through space. This function accounts for the wavelike behavior of matter, such as the diffraction patterns formed by light or electrons passing through a diffraction grating. On the other hand, any given wave function corresponding to a particle has unique values for each point in space and time. These values in turn can be used to calculate the probability that the particle will be detected at any given region in space and time. This aspect of the wave function brings out the particlelike behavior of the matter's building blocks: the matter will be observed as particles in distinct positions. Thanks to the wave function, both the wave and particle properties of matter can be described without contradiction.

xerophyte (zîr′ə-fīt′)

a plant that is adapted to an arid environment.

Many xerophytes have specialized tissues (usually cells that do not perform photosynthesis) for storing water, such as the thick, fleshly leaves of the plants called *succulents.* Among members of the cactus family, the large, thick, green parts are stems adapted as water-storage organs, while the spines are in fact highly modified leaves. Other xerophytes have thin, narrow leaves or woolly coverings for minimizing water loss.

One significant way plants lose water is through their *stomata,* the small holes in their leaves and stems, that allow them to take in carbon dioxide (CO_2) needed for photosynthesis, and vent excess oxygen produced as waste. Although loss of water through the stomata poses no problem for plants living in water or waterlogged environments (*hydrophytes*), or those living in conditions that are neither very wet nor very dry (*mesophytes*), xerophytes have evolved ways to minimize such water loss. Xerophyte leaves have abundant stomata that open to maximize gas exchange when wa-

ALOE VERA
a xerophyte

ter is available and close at other times. Their stomata are often recessed in depressions, which are covered with fine hairs to help trap moisture in the air. Some families of xerophytes have evolved a special form of photosynthesis. They absorb CO_2 at night through their stomata, when temperatures are lower and the relative humidity higher. These plants can store large amounts of CO_2 in a special chemical compound, which during the daytime is converted back into CO_2 for use in photosynthesis. In this way, these xerophytes can perform photosynthesis without exchanging gases through their stomata, which are closed during the daylight hours to save water.

[Greek *xēros*, dry + *phyton*, plant (from *phuein*, to bring forth, produce, spring up, become, from Proto-Indo-European *bheu-*, also the source of the English verb *be*).]

99 yolk

1. *The rounded mass of protein and fat, surrounded by the albumen (the egg white) and often yellow or orange in color, found in the egg of a bird or reptile and serving as the primary source of nourishment for the embryo.* **2.** *The corresponding nutritive portion of the eggs of other animals.*

The yolk of one the unfertilized hen's eggs that we buy in the supermarket is in origin a single cell. Despite its size, it is bounded by a single cellular membrane. The formation of this enormous cell begins with a reproductive cell within the hen's ovary. The cell is enlarged very rapidly with fats and proteins, and after enlargement the nucleus of the cell lies near the cell's outer surface. When this enormous cell is released from the ovary into a canal called an oviduct, it is among the largest cellular structures in the world. Fertilization may occur if the cell encounters sperm and the nucleus of one of the sperm unites with the nucleus of the female reproductive cell. Cell division of the resulting embryo then begins, resulting in a multicellular organism, and the yolk ultimately gets separated from the developing embryo. Ostrich eggs can be 6 inches (15 cm) tall and 5 inches (12.5 cm) across and weigh several pounds, and when considered as a single cellular structure, the yolk of an ostrich egg is by volume the largest cell produced by any living organism. An extinct bird of Madagascar, *Aepyornis* or the elephant bird, laid eggs that were many times larger than an ostrich's, and by volume, their yolks were probably the largest cells ever to have existed on the earth.

[From Old English *geolca*, from *geolu*, yellow.]

zero

A number that when added to another number leaves the original number unchanged.

Although the origin of zero is controversial, some historians believe that it was first used by the Babylonians about 500 BC. In the 6th century, it was discovered by mathematicians in India and China, and 700 years later, it reached Europe by way of the Arabs. Zero provides a way to represent mathematically that there is *none* of something. This makes zero useful as a position holder in the system known as positional notation, the sort of notation we normally use. In the way we write the number 203, for example, the order of the digits tells us that there are two hundreds, no tens, and three ones, and the sum of those values is the value of the number. Scientists use the term *absolute zero* (0 kelvin) to refer to the lowest possible temperature of a substance, the temperature at which no heat can be extracted from it.

[From Italian *zero*, alteration of Medieval Latin *zephirum*, from Arabic *ṣifr*, nothing (translation of Sanskrit *śūnyam*, void, zero), from *ṣafira*, to be empty, from the Proto-Semitic root **ṣpr*.]